C-574 CAREER EXAMINATION SERIES

This is your
PASSBOOK for...

Parole Officer

Test Preparation Study Guide
Questions & Answers

COPYRIGHT NOTICE

This book is SOLELY intended for, is sold ONLY to, and its use is RESTRICTED to individual, bona fide applicants or candidates who qualify by virtue of having seriously filed applications for appropriate license, certificate, professional and/or promotional advancement, higher school matriculation, scholarship, or other legitimate requirements of education and/or governmental authorities.

This book is NOT intended for use, class instruction, tutoring, training, duplication, copying, reprinting, excerption, or adaptation, etc., by:

1) Other publishers
2) Proprietors and/or Instructors of "Coaching" and/or Preparatory Courses
3) Personnel and/or Training Divisions of commercial, industrial, and governmental organizations
4) Schools, colleges, or universities and/or their departments and staffs, including teachers and other personnel
5) Testing Agencies or Bureaus
6) Study groups which seek by the purchase of a single volume to copy and/or duplicate and/or adapt this material for use by the group as a whole without having purchased individual volumes for each of the members of the group
7) Et al.

Such persons would be in violation of appropriate Federal and State statutes.

PROVISION OF LICENSING AGREEMENTS – Recognized educational, commercial, industrial, and governmental institutions and organizations, and others legitimately engaged in educational pursuits, including training, testing, and measurement activities, may address request for a licensing agreement to the copyright owners, who will determine whether, and under what conditions, including fees and charges, the materials in this book may be used them. In other words, a licensing facility exists for the legitimate use of the material in this book on other than an individual basis. However, it is asseverated and affirmed here that the material in this book CANNOT be used without the receipt of the express permission of such a licensing agreement from the Publishers. Inquiries re licensing should be addressed to the company, attention rights and permissions department.

All rights reserved, including the right of reproduction in whole or in part, in any form or by any means, electronic or mechanical, including photocopying, recording, or by any information storage and retrieval system, without permission in writing from the Publisher.

Copyright © 2024 by
National Learning Corporation

212 Michael Drive, Syosset, NY 11791
(516) 921-8888 • www.passbooks.com
E-mail: info@passbooks.com

PASSBOOK® SERIES

THE *PASSBOOK® SERIES* has been created to prepare applicants and candidates for the ultimate academic battlefield – the examination room.

At some time in our lives, each and every one of us may be required to take an examination – for validation, matriculation, admission, qualification, registration, certification, or licensure.

Based on the assumption that every applicant or candidate has met the basic formal educational standards, has taken the required number of courses, and read the necessary texts, the *PASSBOOK® SERIES* furnishes the one special preparation which may assure passing with confidence, instead of failing with insecurity. Examination questions – together with answers – are furnished as the basic vehicle for study so that the mysteries of the examination and its compounding difficulties may be eliminated or diminished by a sure method.

This book is meant to help you pass your examination provided that you qualify and are serious in your objective.

The entire field is reviewed through the huge store of content information which is succinctly presented through a provocative and challenging approach – the question-and-answer method.

A climate of success is established by furnishing the correct answers at the end of each test.

You soon learn to recognize types of questions, forms of questions, and patterns of questioning. You may even begin to anticipate expected outcomes.

You perceive that many questions are repeated or adapted so that you can gain acute insights, which may enable you to score many sure points.

You learn how to confront new questions, or types of questions, and to attack them confidently and work out the correct answers.

You note objectives and emphases, and recognize pitfalls and dangers, so that you may make positive educational adjustments.

Moreover, you are kept fully informed in relation to new concepts, methods, practices, and directions in the field.

You discover that you are actually taking the examination all the time: you are preparing for the examination by "taking" an examination, not by reading extraneous and/or supererogatory textbooks.

In short, this PASSBOOK®, used directedly, should be an important factor in helping you to pass your test.

PAROLE OFFICER

DUTIES

Under general supervision, a Parole Officer makes investigations of inmates eligible for release on parole and does social casework and community protection in the supervision and guidance of parolees. He counsels inmates and investigates their prospective homes, employment, and general environment. He secures, for the Parole Board, information regarding inmates' criminal records, conduct, and other pertinent information. He supervises persons released on parole and assists parolees in their rehabilitation. He investigates employment opportunities and arranges for placement of parolees. He maintains case records and makes reports, interprets the work of the Division of Parole in the community, and may act as liaison between the institution and parolee in preparing inmates for release.

As a Parole Officer, you will be trained in the handling and discharge of firearms, and work with offenders who have histories of committing violent crimes, including sex offenders, and who have various issues such as substance abuse, mental health, domestic violence, and gang involvement. This work will require the development and implementation of appropriate treatment services. Responsibilities also include: working with community providers and law enforcement agencies; the arrest and custody (including transportation) of offenders; field visits to the residences, programs, and places of employment of offenders; entering case contact notes into a computer; preparing written reports and testifying at parole hearings.

Also as a Parole Officer, you would typically be assigned to a Field Parole Office in one of several geographic regions around the state, provide supervision and guidance to an assigned caseload of releasees from state and local correctional facilities, and help releasees comply with the terms and conditions of their release. You would perform both social work and law enforcement functions. You would work with community-based organizations to deliver needed services to an offender population under court-imposed sentences and place releasees under arrest when necessary. You may be assigned to work with juvenile offenders and work releasees.

SCOPE OF THE EXAMINATION:

The multiple-choice written test will cover knowledge, skills, and/or abilities in such areas as:
1. **Preparing written material** - These questions test for the ability to write the kinds of reports and correspondence required in criminal justice settings such as probation and parole. Some questions test for the ability to present information clearly and accurately. Others test for the ability to organize paragraphs logically and comprehensibly.
2. **Principles and practices of offender counseling and supervision** - These questions test for the knowledge and application of principles and practices of offender counseling and supervision in a law enforcement setting. Questions present situations typically encountered while establishing and maintaining working relationships with offenders, such as obtaining information from offenders, exploring offenders' social, psychological, or legal problems, and supervising offender rehabilitation. Candidates will be required to choose the best analysis of, solution to, or approach for handling the problem described. Specific knowledge of laws, rules, regulations, or procedures regarding offender counseling and supervision is not required to answer these questions.

HOW TO TAKE A TEST

I. YOU MUST PASS AN EXAMINATION

A. WHAT EVERY CANDIDATE SHOULD KNOW

Examination applicants often ask us for help in preparing for the written test. What can I study in advance? What kinds of questions will be asked? How will the test be given? How will the papers be graded?

As an applicant for a civil service examination, you may be wondering about some of these things. Our purpose here is to suggest effective methods of advance study and to describe civil service examinations.

Your chances for success on this examination can be increased if you know how to prepare. Those "pre-examination jitters" can be reduced if you know what to expect. You can even experience an adventure in good citizenship if you know why civil service exams are given.

B. WHY ARE CIVIL SERVICE EXAMINATIONS GIVEN?

Civil service examinations are important to you in two ways. As a citizen, you want public jobs filled by employees who know how to do their work. As a job seeker, you want a fair chance to compete for that job on an equal footing with other candidates. The best-known means of accomplishing this two-fold goal is the competitive examination.

Exams are widely publicized throughout the nation. They may be administered for jobs in federal, state, city, municipal, town or village governments or agencies.

Any citizen may apply, with some limitations, such as the age or residence of applicants. Your experience and education may be reviewed to see whether you meet the requirements for the particular examination. When these requirements exist, they are reasonable and applied consistently to all applicants. Thus, a competitive examination may cause you some uneasiness now, but it is your privilege and safeguard.

C. HOW ARE CIVIL SERVICE EXAMS DEVELOPED?

Examinations are carefully written by trained technicians who are specialists in the field known as "psychological measurement," in consultation with recognized authorities in the field of work that the test will cover. These experts recommend the subject matter areas or skills to be tested; only those knowledges or skills important to your success on the job are included. The most reliable books and source materials available are used as references. Together, the experts and technicians judge the difficulty level of the questions.

Test technicians know how to phrase questions so that the problem is clearly stated. Their ethics do not permit "trick" or "catch" questions. Questions may have been tried out on sample groups, or subjected to statistical analysis, to determine their usefulness.

Written tests are often used in combination with performance tests, ratings of training and experience, and oral interviews. All of these measures combine to form the best-known means of finding the right person for the right job.

II. HOW TO PASS THE WRITTEN TEST

A. NATURE OF THE EXAMINATION

To prepare intelligently for civil service examinations, you should know how they differ from school examinations you have taken. In school you were assigned certain definite pages to read or subjects to cover. The examination questions were quite detailed and usually emphasized memory. Civil service exams, on the other hand, try to discover your present ability to perform the duties of a position, plus your potentiality to learn these duties. In other words, a civil service exam attempts to predict how successful you will be. Questions cover such a broad area that they cannot be as minute and detailed as school exam questions.

In the public service similar kinds of work, or positions, are grouped together in one "class." This process is known as *position-classification*. All the positions in a class are paid according to the salary range for that class. One class title covers all of these positions, and they are all tested by the same examination.

B. FOUR BASIC STEPS

1) Study the announcement

How, then, can you know what subjects to study? Our best answer is: "Learn as much as possible about the class of positions for which you've applied." The exam will test the knowledge, skills and abilities needed to do the work.

Your most valuable source of information about the position you want is the official exam announcement. This announcement lists the training and experience qualifications. Check these standards and apply only if you come reasonably close to meeting them.

The brief description of the position in the examination announcement offers some clues to the subjects which will be tested. Think about the job itself. Review the duties in your mind. Can you perform them, or are there some in which you are rusty? Fill in the blank spots in your preparation.

Many jurisdictions preview the written test in the exam announcement by including a section called "Knowledge and Abilities Required," "Scope of the Examination," or some similar heading. Here you will find out specifically what fields will be tested.

2) Review your own background

Once you learn in general what the position is all about, and what you need to know to do the work, ask yourself which subjects you already know fairly well and which need improvement. You may wonder whether to concentrate on improving your strong areas or on building some background in your fields of weakness. When the announcement has specified "some knowledge" or "considerable knowledge," or has used adjectives like "beginning principles of…" or "advanced … methods," you can get a clue as to the number and difficulty of questions to be asked in any given field. More questions, and hence broader coverage, would be included for those subjects which are more important in the work. Now weigh your strengths and weaknesses against the job requirements and prepare accordingly.

3) Determine the level of the position

Another way to tell how intensively you should prepare is to understand the level of the job for which you are applying. Is it the entering level? In other words, is this the position in which beginners in a field of work are hired? Or is it an intermediate or advanced level? Sometimes this is indicated by such words as "Junior" or "Senior" in the class title. Other jurisdictions use Roman numerals to designate the level – Clerk I, Clerk II, for example. The word "Supervisor" sometimes appears in the title. If the level is not indicated by the title, check the description of duties. Will you be working under very close supervision, or will you have responsibility for independent decisions in this work?

4) Choose appropriate study materials

Now that you know the subjects to be examined and the relative amount of each subject to be covered, you can choose suitable study materials. For beginning level jobs, or even advanced ones, if you have a pronounced weakness in some aspect of your training, read a modern, standard textbook in that field. Be sure it is up to date and has general coverage. Such books are normally available at your library, and the librarian will be glad to help you locate one. For entry-level positions, questions of appropriate difficulty are chosen – neither highly advanced questions, nor those too simple. Such questions require careful thought but not advanced training.

If the position for which you are applying is technical or advanced, you will read more advanced, specialized material. If you are already familiar with the basic principles of your field, elementary textbooks would waste your time. Concentrate on advanced textbooks and technical periodicals. Think through the concepts and review difficult problems in your field.

These are all general sources. You can get more ideas on your own initiative, following these leads. For example, training manuals and publications of the government agency which employs workers in your field can be useful, particularly for technical and professional positions. A letter or visit to the government department involved may result in more specific study suggestions, and certainly will provide you with a more definite idea of the exact nature of the position you are seeking.

III. KINDS OF TESTS

Tests are used for purposes other than measuring knowledge and ability to perform specified duties. For some positions, it is equally important to test ability to make adjustments to new situations or to profit from training. In others, basic mental abilities not dependent on information are essential. Questions which test these things may not appear as pertinent to the duties of the position as those which test for knowledge and information. Yet they are often highly important parts of a fair examination. For very general questions, it is almost impossible to help you direct your study efforts. What we can do is to point out some of the more common of these general abilities needed in public service positions and describe some typical questions.

1) General information

Broad, general information has been found useful for predicting job success in some kinds of work. This is tested in a variety of ways, from vocabulary lists to questions about current events. Basic background in some field of work, such as sociology or economics, may be sampled in a group of questions. Often these are principles which have become familiar to most persons through exposure rather than through formal training. It is difficult to advise you how to study for these questions; being alert to the world around you is our best suggestion.

2) Verbal ability

An example of an ability needed in many positions is verbal or language ability. Verbal ability is, in brief, the ability to use and understand words. Vocabulary and grammar tests are typical measures of this ability. Reading comprehension or paragraph interpretation questions are common in many kinds of civil service tests. You are given a paragraph of written material and asked to find its central meaning.

3) Numerical ability

Number skills can be tested by the familiar arithmetic problem, by checking paired lists of numbers to see which are alike and which are different, or by interpreting charts and graphs. In the latter test, a graph may be printed in the test booklet which you are asked to use as the basis for answering questions.

4) Observation

A popular test for law-enforcement positions is the observation test. A picture is shown to you for several minutes, then taken away. Questions about the picture test your ability to observe both details and larger elements.

5) Following directions

In many positions in the public service, the employee must be able to carry out written instructions dependably and accurately. You may be given a chart with several columns, each column listing a variety of information. The questions require you to carry out directions involving the information given in the chart.

6) Skills and aptitudes

Performance tests effectively measure some manual skills and aptitudes. When the skill is one in which you are trained, such as typing or shorthand, you can practice. These tests are often very much like those given in business school or high school courses. For many of the other skills and aptitudes, however, no short-time preparation can be made. Skills and abilities natural to you or that you have developed throughout your lifetime are being tested.

Many of the general questions just described provide all the data needed to answer the questions and ask you to use your reasoning ability to find the answers. Your best preparation for these tests, as well as for tests of facts and ideas, is to be at your physical and mental best. You, no doubt, have your own methods of getting into an exam-taking mood and keeping "in shape." The next section lists some ideas on this subject.

IV. KINDS OF QUESTIONS

Only rarely is the "essay" question, which you answer in narrative form, used in civil service tests. Civil service tests are usually of the short-answer type. Full instructions for answering these questions will be given to you at the examination. But in case this is your first experience with short-answer questions and separate answer sheets, here is what you need to know:

1) **Multiple-choice Questions**

Most popular of the short-answer questions is the "multiple choice" or "best answer" question. It can be used, for example, to test for factual knowledge, ability to solve problems or judgment in meeting situations found at work.

A multiple-choice question is normally one of three types—
- It can begin with an incomplete statement followed by several possible endings. You are to find the one ending which *best* completes the statement, although some of the others may not be entirely wrong.
- It can also be a complete statement in the form of a question which is answered by choosing one of the statements listed.

- It can be in the form of a problem – again you select the best answer.

Here is an example of a multiple-choice question with a discussion which should give you some clues as to the method for choosing the right answer:

When an employee has a complaint about his assignment, the action which will *best* help him overcome his difficulty is to
- A. discuss his difficulty with his coworkers
- B. take the problem to the head of the organization
- C. take the problem to the person who gave him the assignment
- D. say nothing to anyone about his complaint

In answering this question, you should study each of the choices to find which is best. Consider choice "A" – Certainly an employee may discuss his complaint with fellow employees, but no change or improvement can result, and the complaint remains unresolved. Choice "B" is a poor choice since the head of the organization probably does not know what assignment you have been given, and taking your problem to him is known as "going over the head" of the supervisor. The supervisor, or person who made the assignment, is the person who can clarify it or correct any injustice. Choice "C" is, therefore, correct. To say nothing, as in choice "D," is unwise. Supervisors have and interest in knowing the problems employees are facing, and the employee is seeking a solution to his problem.

2) True/False Questions

The "true/false" or "right/wrong" form of question is sometimes used. Here a complete statement is given. Your job is to decide whether the statement is right or wrong.

SAMPLE: A roaming cell-phone call to a nearby city costs less than a non-roaming call to a distant city.

This statement is wrong, or false, since roaming calls are more expensive.

This is not a complete list of all possible question forms, although most of the others are variations of these common types. You will always get complete directions for answering questions. Be sure you understand *how* to mark your answers – ask questions until you do.

V. RECORDING YOUR ANSWERS

Computer terminals are used more and more today for many different kinds of exams.

For an examination with very few applicants, you may be told to record your answers in the test booklet itself. Separate answer sheets are much more common. If this separate answer sheet is to be scored by machine – and this is often the case – it is highly important that you mark your answers correctly in order to get credit.

An electronic scoring machine is often used in civil service offices because of the speed with which papers can be scored. Machine-scored answer sheets must be marked with a pencil, which will be given to you. This pencil has a high graphite content which responds to the electronic scoring machine. As a matter of fact, stray dots may register as answers, so do not let your pencil rest on the answer sheet while you are pondering the correct answer. Also, if your pencil lead breaks or is otherwise defective, ask for another.

Since the answer sheet will be dropped in a slot in the scoring machine, be careful not to bend the corners or get the paper crumpled.

The answer sheet normally has five vertical columns of numbers, with 30 numbers to a column. These numbers correspond to the question numbers in your test booklet. After each number, going across the page are four or five pairs of dotted lines. These short dotted lines have small letters or numbers above them. The first two pairs may also have a "T" or "F" above the letters. This indicates that the first two pairs only are to be used if the questions are of the true-false type. If the questions are multiple choice, disregard the "T" and "F" and pay attention only to the small letters or numbers.

Answer your questions in the manner of the sample that follows:

32. The largest city in the United States is
    A. Washington, D.C.
    B. New York City
    C. Chicago
    D. Detroit
    E. San Francisco

1) Choose the answer you think is best. (New York City is the largest, so "B" is correct.)
2) Find the row of dotted lines numbered the same as the question you are answering. (Find row number 32)
3) Find the pair of dotted lines corresponding to the answer. (Find the pair of lines under the mark "B.")
4) Make a solid black mark between the dotted lines.

VI. BEFORE THE TEST

Common sense will help you find procedures to follow to get ready for an examination. Too many of us, however, overlook these sensible measures. Indeed, nervousness and fatigue have been found to be the most serious reasons why applicants fail to do their best on civil service tests. Here is a list of reminders:

- Begin your preparation early – Don't wait until the last minute to go scurrying around for books and materials or to find out what the position is all about.
- Prepare continuously – An hour a night for a week is better than an all-night cram session. This has been definitely established. What is more, a night a week for a month will return better dividends than crowding your study into a shorter period of time.
- Locate the place of the exam – You have been sent a notice telling you when and where to report for the examination. If the location is in a different town or otherwise unfamiliar to you, it would be well to inquire the best route and learn something about the building.
- Relax the night before the test – Allow your mind to rest. Do not study at all that night. Plan some mild recreation or diversion; then go to bed early and get a good night's sleep.
- Get up early enough to make a leisurely trip to the place for the test – This way unforeseen events, traffic snarls, unfamiliar buildings, etc. will not upset you.
- Dress comfortably – A written test is not a fashion show. You will be known by number and not by name, so wear something comfortable.

- Leave excess paraphernalia at home – Shopping bags and odd bundles will get in your way. You need bring only the items mentioned in the official notice you received; usually everything you need is provided. Do not bring reference books to the exam. They will only confuse those last minutes and be taken away from you when in the test room.
- Arrive somewhat ahead of time – If because of transportation schedules you must get there very early, bring a newspaper or magazine to take your mind off yourself while waiting.
- Locate the examination room – When you have found the proper room, you will be directed to the seat or part of the room where you will sit. Sometimes you are given a sheet of instructions to read while you are waiting. Do not fill out any forms until you are told to do so; just read them and be prepared.
- Relax and prepare to listen to the instructions
- If you have any physical problem that may keep you from doing your best, be sure to tell the test administrator. If you are sick or in poor health, you really cannot do your best on the exam. You can come back and take the test some other time.

VII. AT THE TEST

The day of the test is here and you have the test booklet in your hand. The temptation to get going is very strong. Caution! There is more to success than knowing the right answers. You must know how to identify your papers and understand variations in the type of short-answer question used in this particular examination. Follow these suggestions for maximum results from your efforts:

1) Cooperate with the monitor

The test administrator has a duty to create a situation in which you can be as much at ease as possible. He will give instructions, tell you when to begin, check to see that you are marking your answer sheet correctly, and so on. He is not there to guard you, although he will see that your competitors do not take unfair advantage. He wants to help you do your best.

2) Listen to all instructions

Don't jump the gun! Wait until you understand all directions. In most civil service tests you get more time than you need to answer the questions. So don't be in a hurry. Read each word of instructions until you clearly understand the meaning. Study the examples, listen to all announcements and follow directions. Ask questions if you do not understand what to do.

3) Identify your papers

Civil service exams are usually identified by number only. You will be assigned a number; you must not put your name on your test papers. Be sure to copy your number correctly. Since more than one exam may be given, copy your exact examination title.

4) Plan your time

Unless you are told that a test is a "speed" or "rate of work" test, speed itself is usually not important. Time enough to answer all the questions will be provided, but this does not mean that you have all day. An overall time limit has been set. Divide the total time (in minutes) by the number of questions to determine the approximate time you have for each question.

5) Do not linger over difficult questions

If you come across a difficult question, mark it with a paper clip (useful to have along) and come back to it when you have been through the booklet. One caution if you do this – be sure to skip a number on your answer sheet as well. Check often to be sure that you have not lost your place and that you are marking in the row numbered the same as the question you are answering.

6) Read the questions

Be sure you know what the question asks! Many capable people are unsuccessful because they failed to *read* the questions correctly.

7) Answer all questions

Unless you have been instructed that a penalty will be deducted for incorrect answers, it is better to guess than to omit a question.

8) Speed tests

It is often better NOT to guess on speed tests. It has been found that on timed tests people are tempted to spend the last few seconds before time is called in marking answers at random – without even reading them – in the hope of picking up a few extra points. To discourage this practice, the instructions may warn you that your score will be "corrected" for guessing. That is, a penalty will be applied. The incorrect answers will be deducted from the correct ones, or some other penalty formula will be used.

9) Review your answers

If you finish before time is called, go back to the questions you guessed or omitted to give them further thought. Review other answers if you have time.

10) Return your test materials

If you are ready to leave before others have finished or time is called, take ALL your materials to the monitor and leave quietly. Never take any test material with you. The monitor can discover whose papers are not complete, and taking a test booklet may be grounds for disqualification.

VIII. EXAMINATION TECHNIQUES

1) Read the general instructions carefully. These are usually printed on the first page of the exam booklet. As a rule, these instructions refer to the timing of the examination; the fact that you should not start work until the signal and must stop work at a signal, etc. If there are any *special* instructions, such as a choice of questions to be answered, make sure that you note this instruction carefully.

2) When you are ready to start work on the examination, that is as soon as the signal has been given, read the instructions to each question booklet, underline any key words or phrases, such as *least, best, outline, describe* and the like. In this way you will tend to answer as requested rather than discover on reviewing your paper that you *listed without describing*, that you selected the *worst* choice rather than the *best* choice, etc.

3) If the examination is of the objective or multiple-choice type – that is, each question will also give a series of possible answers: A, B, C or D, and you are called upon to select the best answer and write the letter next to that answer on your answer paper – it is advisable to start answering each question in turn. There may be anywhere from 50 to 100 such questions in the three or four hours allotted and you can see how much time would be taken if you read through all the questions before beginning to answer any. Furthermore, if you come across a question or group of questions which you know would be difficult to answer, it would undoubtedly affect your handling of all the other questions.

4) If the examination is of the essay type and contains but a few questions, it is a moot point as to whether you should read all the questions before starting to answer any one. Of course, if you are given a choice – say five out of seven and the like – then it is essential to read all the questions so you can eliminate the two that are most difficult. If, however, you are asked to answer all the questions, there may be danger in trying to answer the easiest one first because you may find that you will spend too much time on it. The best technique is to answer the first question, then proceed to the second, etc.

5) Time your answers. Before the exam begins, write down the time it started, then add the time allowed for the examination and write down the time it must be completed, then divide the time available somewhat as follows:
    - If 3-1/2 hours are allowed, that would be 210 minutes. If you have 80 objective-type questions, that would be an average of 2-1/2 minutes per question. Allow yourself no more than 2 minutes per question, or a total of 160 minutes, which will permit about 50 minutes to review.
    - If for the time allotment of 210 minutes there are 7 essay questions to answer, that would average about 30 minutes a question. Give yourself only 25 minutes per question so that you have about 35 minutes to review.

6) The most important instruction is to *read each question* and make sure you know what is wanted. The second most important instruction is to *time yourself properly* so that you answer every question. The third most important instruction is to *answer every question*. Guess if you have to but include something for each question. Remember that you will receive no credit for a blank and will probably receive some credit if you write something in answer to an essay question. If you guess a letter – say "B" for a multiple-choice question – you may have guessed right. If you leave a blank as an answer to a multiple-choice question, the examiners may respect your feelings but it will not add a point to your score. Some exams may penalize you for wrong answers, so in such cases *only*, you may not want to guess unless you have some basis for your answer.

7) Suggestions
    a. Objective-type questions
        1. Examine the question booklet for proper sequence of pages and questions
        2. Read all instructions carefully
        3. Skip any question which seems too difficult; return to it after all other questions have been answered
        4. Apportion your time properly; do not spend too much time on any single question or group of questions

5. Note and underline key words – *all, most, fewest, least, best, worst, same, opposite*, etc.
6. Pay particular attention to negatives
7. Note unusual option, e.g., unduly long, short, complex, different or similar in content to the body of the question
8. Observe the use of "hedging" words – *probably, may, most likely*, etc.
9. Make sure that your answer is put next to the same number as the question
10. Do not second-guess unless you have good reason to believe the second answer is definitely more correct
11. Cross out original answer if you decide another answer is more accurate; do not erase until you are ready to hand your paper in
12. Answer all questions; guess unless instructed otherwise
13. Leave time for review

b. Essay questions
1. Read each question carefully
2. Determine exactly what is wanted. Underline key words or phrases.
3. Decide on outline or paragraph answer
4. Include many different points and elements unless asked to develop any one or two points or elements
5. Show impartiality by giving pros and cons unless directed to select one side only
6. Make and write down any assumptions you find necessary to answer the questions
7. Watch your English, grammar, punctuation and choice of words
8. Time your answers; don't crowd material

8) Answering the essay question

Most essay questions can be answered by framing the specific response around several key words or ideas. Here are a few such key words or ideas:

M's: manpower, materials, methods, money, management
P's: purpose, program, policy, plan, procedure, practice, problems, pitfalls, personnel, public relations

a. Six basic steps in handling problems:
1. Preliminary plan and background development
2. Collect information, data and facts
3. Analyze and interpret information, data and facts
4. Analyze and develop solutions as well as make recommendations
5. Prepare report and sell recommendations
6. Install recommendations and follow up effectiveness

b. Pitfalls to avoid
1. *Taking things for granted* – A statement of the situation does not necessarily imply that each of the elements is necessarily true; for example, a complaint may be invalid and biased so that all that can be taken for granted is that a complaint has been registered

2. *Considering only one side of a situation* – Wherever possible, indicate several alternatives and then point out the reasons you selected the best one
3. *Failing to indicate follow up* – Whenever your answer indicates action on your part, make certain that you will take proper follow-up action to see how successful your recommendations, procedures or actions turn out to be
4. *Taking too long in answering any single question* – Remember to time your answers properly

IX. AFTER THE TEST

Scoring procedures differ in detail among civil service jurisdictions although the general principles are the same. Whether the papers are hand-scored or graded by machine we have described, they are nearly always graded by number. That is, the person who marks the paper knows only the number – never the name – of the applicant. Not until all the papers have been graded will they be matched with names. If other tests, such as training and experience or oral interview ratings have been given, scores will be combined. Different parts of the examination usually have different weights. For example, the written test might count 60 percent of the final grade, and a rating of training and experience 40 percent. In many jurisdictions, veterans will have a certain number of points added to their grades.

After the final grade has been determined, the names are placed in grade order and an eligible list is established. There are various methods for resolving ties between those who get the same final grade – probably the most common is to place first the name of the person whose application was received first. Job offers are made from the eligible list in the order the names appear on it. You will be notified of your grade and your rank as soon as all these computations have been made. This will be done as rapidly as possible.

People who are found to meet the requirements in the announcement are called "eligibles." Their names are put on a list of eligible candidates. An eligible's chances of getting a job depend on how high he stands on this list and how fast agencies are filling jobs from the list.

When a job is to be filled from a list of eligibles, the agency asks for the names of people on the list of eligibles for that job. When the civil service commission receives this request, it sends to the agency the names of the three people highest on this list. Or, if the job to be filled has specialized requirements, the office sends the agency the names of the top three persons who meet these requirements from the general list.

The appointing officer makes a choice from among the three people whose names were sent to him. If the selected person accepts the appointment, the names of the others are put back on the list to be considered for future openings.

That is the rule in hiring from all kinds of eligible lists, whether they are for typist, carpenter, chemist, or something else. For every vacancy, the appointing officer has his choice of any one of the top three eligibles on the list. This explains why the person whose name is on top of the list sometimes does not get an appointment when some of the persons lower on the list do. If the appointing officer chooses the second or third eligible, the No. 1 eligible does not get a job at once, but stays on the list until he is appointed or the list is terminated.

X. HOW TO PASS THE INTERVIEW TEST

The examination for which you applied requires an oral interview test. You have already taken the written test and you are now being called for the interview test – the final part of the formal examination.

You may think that it is not possible to prepare for an interview test and that there are no procedures to follow during an interview. Our purpose is to point out some things you can do in advance that will help you and some good rules to follow and pitfalls to avoid while you are being interviewed.

What is an interview supposed to test?

The written examination is designed to test the technical knowledge and competence of the candidate; the oral is designed to evaluate intangible qualities, not readily measured otherwise, and to establish a list showing the relative fitness of each candidate – as measured against his competitors – for the position sought. Scoring is not on the basis of "right" and "wrong," but on a sliding scale of values ranging from "not passable" to "outstanding." As a matter of fact, it is possible to achieve a relatively low score without a single "incorrect" answer because of evident weakness in the qualities being measured.

Occasionally, an examination may consist entirely of an oral test – either an individual or a group oral. In such cases, information is sought concerning the technical knowledges and abilities of the candidate, since there has been no written examination for this purpose. More commonly, however, an oral test is used to supplement a written examination.

Who conducts interviews?

The composition of oral boards varies among different jurisdictions. In nearly all, a representative of the personnel department serves as chairman. One of the members of the board may be a representative of the department in which the candidate would work. In some cases, "outside experts" are used, and, frequently, a businessman or some other representative of the general public is asked to serve. Labor and management or other special groups may be represented. The aim is to secure the services of experts in the appropriate field.

However the board is composed, it is a good idea (and not at all improper or unethical) to ascertain in advance of the interview who the members are and what groups they represent. When you are introduced to them, you will have some idea of their backgrounds and interests, and at least you will not stutter and stammer over their names.

What should be done before the interview?

While knowledge about the board members is useful and takes some of the surprise element out of the interview, there is other preparation which is more substantive. It *is* possible to prepare for an oral interview – in several ways:

1) Keep a copy of your application and review it carefully before the interview

This may be the only document before the oral board, and the starting point of the interview. Know what education and experience you have listed there, and the sequence and dates of all of it. Sometimes the board will ask you to review the highlights of your experience for them; you should not have to hem and haw doing it.

2) Study the class specification and the examination announcement

Usually, the oral board has one or both of these to guide them. The qualities, characteristics or knowledges required by the position sought are stated in these documents. They offer valuable clues as to the nature of the oral interview. For example, if the job involves supervisory responsibilities, the announcement will usually indicate that knowledge of modern supervisory methods and the qualifications of the candidate as a supervisor will be tested. If so, you can expect such questions, frequently in the form of a hypothetical situation which you are expected to solve. NEVER go into an oral without knowledge of the duties and responsibilities of the job you seek.

3) Think through each qualification required

Try to visualize the kind of questions you would ask if you were a board member. How well could you answer them? Try especially to appraise your own knowledge and background in each area, *measured against the job sought*, and identify any areas in which you are weak. Be critical and realistic – do not flatter yourself.

4) Do some general reading in areas in which you feel you may be weak

For example, if the job involves supervision and your past experience has NOT, some general reading in supervisory methods and practices, particularly in the field of human relations, might be useful. Do NOT study agency procedures or detailed manuals. The oral board will be testing your understanding and capacity, not your memory.

5) Get a good night's sleep and watch your general health and mental attitude

You will want a clear head at the interview. Take care of a cold or any other minor ailment, and of course, no hangovers.

What should be done on the day of the interview?

Now comes the day of the interview itself. Give yourself plenty of time to get there. Plan to arrive somewhat ahead of the scheduled time, particularly if your appointment is in the fore part of the day. If a previous candidate fails to appear, the board might be ready for you a bit early. By early afternoon an oral board is almost invariably behind schedule if there are many candidates, and you may have to wait. Take along a book or magazine to read, or your application to review, but leave any extraneous material in the waiting room when you go in for your interview. In any event, relax and compose yourself.

The matter of dress is important. The board is forming impressions about you – from your experience, your manners, your attitude, and your appearance. Give your personal appearance careful attention. Dress your best, but not your flashiest. Choose conservative, appropriate clothing, and be sure it is immaculate. This is a business interview, and your appearance should indicate that you regard it as such. Besides, being well groomed and properly dressed will help boost your confidence.

Sooner or later, someone will call your name and escort you into the interview room. *This is it.* From here on you are on your own. It is too late for any more preparation. But remember, you asked for this opportunity to prove your fitness, and you are here because your request was granted.

What happens when you go in?

The usual sequence of events will be as follows: The clerk (who is often the board stenographer) will introduce you to the chairman of the oral board, who will introduce you to the other members of the board. Acknowledge the introductions before you sit down. Do not be surprised if you find a microphone facing you or a stenotypist sitting by. Oral interviews are usually recorded in the event of an appeal or other review.

Usually the chairman of the board will open the interview by reviewing the highlights of your education and work experience from your application – primarily for the benefit of the other members of the board, as well as to get the material into the record. Do not interrupt or comment unless there is an error or significant misinterpretation; if that is the case, do not hesitate. But do not quibble about insignificant matters. Also, he will usually ask you some question about your education, experience or your present job – partly to get you to start talking and to establish the interviewing "rapport." He may start the actual questioning, or turn it over to one of the other members. Frequently, each member undertakes the questioning on a particular area, one in which he is perhaps most competent, so you can expect each member to participate in the examination. Because time is limited, you may also expect some rather abrupt switches in the direction the questioning takes, so do not be upset by it. Normally, a board member will not pursue a single line of questioning unless he discovers a particular strength or weakness.

After each member has participated, the chairman will usually ask whether any member has any further questions, then will ask you if you have anything you wish to add. Unless you are expecting this question, it may floor you. Worse, it may start you off on an extended, extemporaneous speech. The board is not usually seeking more information. The question is principally to offer you a last opportunity to present further qualifications or to indicate that you have nothing to add. So, if you feel that a significant qualification or characteristic has been overlooked, it is proper to point it out in a sentence or so. Do not compliment the board on the thoroughness of their examination – they have been sketchy, and you know it. If you wish, merely say, "No thank you, I have nothing further to add." This is a point where you can "talk yourself out" of a good impression or fail to present an important bit of information. Remember, *you close the interview yourself*.

The chairman will then say, "That is all, Mr. _____, thank you." Do not be startled; the interview is over, and quicker than you think. Thank him, gather your belongings and take your leave. Save your sigh of relief for the other side of the door.

How to put your best foot forward

Throughout this entire process, you may feel that the board individually and collectively is trying to pierce your defenses, seek out your hidden weaknesses and embarrass and confuse you. Actually, this is not true. They are obliged to make an appraisal of your qualifications for the job you are seeking, and they want to see you in your best light. Remember, they must interview all candidates and a non-cooperative candidate may become a failure in spite of their best efforts to bring out his qualifications. Here are 15 suggestions that will help you:

1) Be natural – Keep your attitude confident, not cocky

If you are not confident that you can do the job, do not expect the board to be. Do not apologize for your weaknesses, try to bring out your strong points. The board is interested in a positive, not negative, presentation. Cockiness will antagonize any board member and make him wonder if you are covering up a weakness by a false show of strength.

2) Get comfortable, but don't lounge or sprawl

Sit erectly but not stiffly. A careless posture may lead the board to conclude that you are careless in other things, or at least that you are not impressed by the importance of the occasion. Either conclusion is natural, even if incorrect. Do not fuss with your clothing, a pencil or an ashtray. Your hands may occasionally be useful to emphasize a point; do not let them become a point of distraction.

3) Do not wisecrack or make small talk

This is a serious situation, and your attitude should show that you consider it as such. Further, the time of the board is limited – they do not want to waste it, and neither should you.

4) Do not exaggerate your experience or abilities

In the first place, from information in the application or other interviews and sources, the board may know more about you than you think. Secondly, you probably will not get away with it. An experienced board is rather adept at spotting such a situation, so do not take the chance.

5) If you know a board member, do not make a point of it, yet do not hide it

Certainly you are not fooling him, and probably not the other members of the board. Do not try to take advantage of your acquaintanceship – it will probably do you little good.

6) Do not dominate the interview

Let the board do that. They will give you the clues – do not assume that you have to do all the talking. Realize that the board has a number of questions to ask you, and do not try to take up all the interview time by showing off your extensive knowledge of the answer to the first one.

7) Be attentive

You only have 20 minutes or so, and you should keep your attention at its sharpest throughout. When a member is addressing a problem or question to you, give him your undivided attention. Address your reply principally to him, but do not exclude the other board members.

8) Do not interrupt

A board member may be stating a problem for you to analyze. He will ask you a question when the time comes. Let him state the problem, and wait for the question.

9) Make sure you understand the question

Do not try to answer until you are sure what the question is. If it is not clear, restate it in your own words or ask the board member to clarify it for you. However, do not haggle about minor elements.

10) Reply promptly but not hastily

A common entry on oral board rating sheets is "candidate responded readily," or "candidate hesitated in replies." Respond as promptly and quickly as you can, but do not jump to a hasty, ill-considered answer.

11) Do not be peremptory in your answers

A brief answer is proper – but do not fire your answer back. That is a losing game from your point of view. The board member can probably ask questions much faster than you can answer them.

12) Do not try to create the answer you think the board member wants

He is interested in what kind of mind you have and how it works – not in playing games. Furthermore, he can usually spot this practice and will actually grade you down on it.

13) Do not switch sides in your reply merely to agree with a board member

Frequently, a member will take a contrary position merely to draw you out and to see if you are willing and able to defend your point of view. Do not start a debate, yet do not surrender a good position. If a position is worth taking, it is worth defending.

14) Do not be afraid to admit an error in judgment if you are shown to be wrong
The board knows that you are forced to reply without any opportunity for careful consideration. Your answer may be demonstrably wrong. If so, admit it and get on with the interview.

15) Do not dwell at length on your present job
The opening question may relate to your present assignment. Answer the question but do not go into an extended discussion. You are being examined for a *new* job, not your present one. As a matter of fact, try to phrase ALL your answers in terms of the job for which you are being examined.

Basis of Rating
Probably you will forget most of these "do's" and "don'ts" when you walk into the oral interview room. Even remembering them all will not ensure you a passing grade. Perhaps you did not have the qualifications in the first place. But remembering them will help you to put your best foot forward, without treading on the toes of the board members.

Rumor and popular opinion to the contrary notwithstanding, an oral board wants you to make the best appearance possible. They know you are under pressure – but they also want to see how you respond to it as a guide to what your reaction would be under the pressures of the job you seek. They will be influenced by the degree of poise you display, the personal traits you show and the manner in which you respond.

ABOUT THIS BOOK

This book contains tests divided into Examination Sections. Go through each test, answering every question in the margin. We have also attached a sample answer sheet at the back of the book that can be removed and used. At the end of each test look at the answer key and check your answers. On the ones you got wrong, look at the right answer choice and learn. Do not fill in the answers first. Do not memorize the questions and answers, but understand the answer and principles involved. On your test, the questions will likely be different from the samples. Questions are changed and new ones added. If you understand these past questions you should have success with any changes that arise. Tests may consist of several types of questions. We have additional books on each subject should more study be advisable or necessary for you. Finally, the more you study, the better prepared you will be. This book is intended to be the last thing you study before you walk into the examination room. Prior study of relevant texts is also recommended. NLC publishes some of these in our Fundamental Series. Knowledge and good sense are important factors in passing your exam. Good luck also helps. So now study this Passbook, absorb the material contained within and take that knowledge into the examination. Then do your best to pass that exam.

EXAMINATION SECTION

EXAMINATION SECTION
TEST 1

DIRECTIONS: Each question or incomplete statement is followed by several suggested answers or completions. Select the one that BEST answers the question or completes the statement. *PRINT THE LETTER OF THE CORRECT ANSWER IN THE SPACE AT THE RIGHT.*

1. The primary aim of the traditional treatment-oriented model of reintegrating offenders is 1.____

    A. the cultivation of remorse and conscience
    B. the establishment of a routine that will limit an offender's behavioral options
    C. long-term change in offender behavior
    D. the creation of an undesignated *buffer* between the offender and potential victims

2. What is the term for a judicial or quasi-judicial proceeding held to determine whether it is appropriate to continue to hold a juvenile in a shelter facility? 2.____

    A. Demand waiver
    B. Detention hearing
    C. Delinquency petition
    D. Detainer warrant

3. Which of the following is considered to be an advantage of indeterminate sentencing in relation to parole? 3.____
   It

    A. forces society to confront the underlying causes of crime
    B. involves concrete, easily followed guidelines for the designation of some offenders as mentally ill
    C. offers maximum protection to society from hard-core recidivists
    D. supplies much positive motivation to prisoners for their own rehabilitation

4. Status offenses that are removed from the jurisdiction of juvenile court or secure-custody facilities are described as 4.____

    A. deinstitutionalized
    B. commutated
    C. desanctioned
    D. readjudicated

5. The most common organizational model for adult paroling authorities is the _____ model. 5.____

    A. institutional
    B. consolidation
    C. intensive
    D. autonomous

6. The substations or satellite offices of regular probation and parole agencies are commonly referred to as 6.____

    A. annexes
    B. PORTs
    C. outreach centers
    D. halfway houses

7. When parole was first practiced in some form in Europe in the 1700s, it was largely instituted in response to 7.____

    A. excessive sentencing by judges
    B. a growing reform movement that emphasized rehabilitation

C. political corruption involved in early release
D. prison overcrowding

8. *Avertable recidivist* is a term that refers to

   A. a new concept based on the correctional goal of offender reintegration into the community
   B. the phenomenon of gradually progressing to more serious forms of offending
   C. an offender who would still have been in prison serving a sentence at a time when a new offense was committed
   D. one who commits a misdemeanor

9. The first true use of parole in the United States occurred in

   A. 1790, in Pennsylvania   B. 1817, in New York
   C. 1846, in Tennessee   D. 1884, in Massachusetts

10. Collectively, probation, diversion, and community-based correctional programs are described as _____ solutions to jail and prison overcrowding.

    A. front-end   B. contractive
    C. halfway   D. nominal

11. Juvenile intensive supervision probation (JISP) programs are typically characterized by each of the following EXCEPT

    A. high levels of offender control
    B. low levels of offender responsibility
    C. frequent checks for arrests, substance abuse, and employment/school attendance
    D. low officer/client caseloads

12. The collective term used for the constraints imposed on some probationers or parolees to increase the restrictiveness or painfulness of probation or parole is

    A. treatment conditions   B. strictures
    C. civil disabilities   D. punitive conditions

13. The MOST reliable indicator of recidivism, as well as the most valid definition of the term, is

    A. revocation or unsatisfactory termination
    B. reconviction
    C. technical rule violations
    D. rearrest

14. Correction officers sometimes attempt to predict the future behavior of inmates based on a class of offenders considered for parole. This process is known as

    A. matching   B. actuarial prediction
    C. anamnestic prediction   D. clinical prediction

15. Currently, the most important factor in parole board decision-making appears to be

    A. the increasing emphasis on public safety
    B. the growth of the community corrections movement

C. prison overcrowding
D. the spread of presumptive sentencing

16. Currently, the federal corrections system grants federal prisoners up to _____ days per year as good-time credit against their original sentence lengths.

   A. 36 B. 54 C. 88 D. 120

17. The functions of most work release programs include
   I. participation in vocational or educational training
   II. provision of food and shelter
   III. promotion of self-respect
   IV. community reintegration

   The CORRECT answer is:

   A. I, II
   B. I, III, IV
   C. II, IV
   D. I, III

18. The Federal Tort Claims Act of 1946 permits

   A. correctional officers and parole or probation supervisors to sue inmates or clients for punitive damages arising from harm associated with the officer/inmate or PO-client relation
   B. victims of crimes to sue the offender for punitive damages arising from the harm associated with the commission of the crime, regardless of criminal conviction
   C. federal prisoners and those under federal parole or probation supervision the right to sue their supervisors and/or administrators for punitive damages arising from harm associated with officer/inmate or PO-client relation
   D. defendants to sue for punitive damages arising from the harm associated with wrongful prosecution

19. Which of the following comparative statements about probation and parole is generally TRUE?

   A. Probation usually has a higher success rate.
   B. Probation is not granted to violent criminals.
   C. Parole has traditionally been more punishment-oriented.
   D. Parole involves a more intensive one-on-one monitoring effort.

20. Which of the following is a basic measure of the occurrence of a crime?

   A. Technical infraction
   B. Expense
   C. Victimization
   D. Increased risk or threat

21. Among corrections professionals, the term *furlough* is often used interchangeably with

   A. conditional prerelease
   B. standard parole
   C. unconditional prerelease
   D. work release

22. What is the term for a parole board decision-making system that emphasizes the functions of parole supervision and management?
   _____ system.

   A. Congregate
   B. Jurist value
   C. Controller value
   D. Specialized caseloads

23. Which of the following is a policy implication involved in the rehabilitation model of probation practice?
    A. Reduced judicial discretion
    B. Mandated sentencing ranges
    C. Decriminalization
    D. Proportional sentencing

24. The portion of a presentence investigation report prepared by a parole officer or agency, in which a description of the offense and the offender is provided, and which culminates in and justifies a recommendation for a specific sentence to be imposed on the offender by the judges, is called the
    A. portrait parle
    B. narrative
    C. needs assessment
    D. presentment

25. Nationwide, approximately what percentage of parole terms currently end in successful completion?
    A. 15
    B. 35
    C. 50
    D. 75

KEY (CORRECT ANSWERS)

1. C
2. B
3. C
4. A
5. D

6. C
7. D
8. C
9. D
10. A

11. B
12. D
13. B
14. B
15. C

16. B
17. B
18. C
19. C
20. C

21. D
22. C
23. C
24. B
25. B

TEST 2

DIRECTIONS: Each question or incomplete statement is followed by several suggested answers or completions. Select the one that BEST answers the question or completes the statement. *PRINT THE LETTER OF THE CORRECT ANSWER IN THE SPACE AT THE RIGHT.*

1. In the _____ model of supervision, the probation/parole officer serves primarily as a counselor, dispensing *treatment* to *clients* in a one-on-one therapeutic relationship. 1.____

   A. justice B. casework C. brokerage D. medical

2. At the departmental level, the most important goal of officers is typically identified as 2.____

   A. successful completion of the parole term
   B. the reintegration of the client
   C. rehabilitation
   D. the safety of the community

3. Evidence or material that demonstrates or supports a defendant's innocence is described as 3.____

   A. exculpatory B. mitigating
   C. injunctive   D. recusive

4. Which of the following is NOT generally perceived to be a difference between modern jails and modern prisons? 4.____

   A. Jails have a greater diversity of inmates.
   B. The physical plants of prisons are in poorer condition.
   C. Jails are not usually partitioned into areas of differing security.
   D. Prison inmate culture is more pronounced and persistent.

5. The United States Supreme Court ruling in the 1983 <u>Bearden v. Georgia</u> case established that 5.____

   A. probationers and parolees are entitled to legal representation at any revocation hearing
   B. a probationer who is indigent may not have probation revoked because of a failure to pay fines or make restitution
   C. the legal procedural requirements for probation revocation are the same as that for parole
   D. judges are not generally obligated to consider alternatives to incarceration before revoking an offender's probation

6. A petty crime, punishable by a fine only, is described as a 6.____

   A. summary offense   B. nugatory offense
   C. status offense   D. misdemeanor

7. Which of the following statements about probationer/parolee rights relative to program conditions is FALSE?

    A. A probationer/parolee who is in custody is not entitled to a Miranda warning.
    B. Search and seizure grounds are less stringent for POs who itend to search a client's home for contraband.
    C. Statements made to a PO during questioning are admissible under almost any circumstances as evidence in court for supporting new criminal cases.
    D. Restitution is a legitimate condition of probation/ parole, but not always an efforceable condition.

8. What is the term for any authorized, unescorted leave from confinement granted for a specific purpose and for a designated time period?

    A. Pass
    B. Release-on-recognizance
    C. Furlough
    D. Parole

9. Which of the following offers the best explanation for why some probation/parole officers choose to overlook certain technical violations by offenders?

    A. The officer has developed a sympathetic attitude toward the offender.
    B. It is not considered evidence of criminal activity.
    C. Reincarceration of the offender may only serve to. aggravate the overcrowding problem.
    D. The violation may have been committed intentionally.

10. Circumstances of a crime that enhance an offender's sentence are described as

    A. aggravating
    B. mitigating
    C. amplifying
    D. augmenting

11. Though community-based corrections programs vary in size and scope, they tend to share common characteristics. Which of the following is NOT one of these?

    A. On-call support services (medical, social, psychological)
    B. Heightened staff accountability to the court concerning offender progress
    C. Centralized control of program resources
    D. 24-hour availability of administrators on premises

12. Which of the following is not considered to be an *intermediate sanction*?

    A. Probation
    B. House arrest
    C. Community service
    D. Restitution

13. Which of the following is NOT typically a goal of home confinement? To

    A. reduce the costs of offender supervision
    B. demonstrate faith in the offender's word
    C. maintain a controlled community presence
    D. enable offenders to assume familial responsibility

14. For most of the current period, beginning in the 1970s, the prevailing philosophy operating in United States corrections has shifted to that of

    A. isolation
    B. rehabilitation
    C. retribution
    D. deterrence

15. The official document that is filed in juvenile courts on the juvenile's behalf, specifying the reasons for the court appearance, is the

    A. conferral   B. bid   C. petition   D. linkage

16. In evaluating a parole program's effectiveness in assessing an offender's suitability for placement, which of the following would be the most appropriate performance indicator?

    A. Number of drug-free and/or alcohol-free days during supervision
    B. Number and type of technical violations during supervision
    C. Accuracy and completeness of presentence investigations
    D. Extent of victim satisfaction with service and department

17. In 1931, a report was released on the status of United States parole practices by the Wickersham Commission, a National Commission on Law Observance and Enforcement. Which of the following were findings of the report?
    I. Victims were dissatisfied with the amount of prison time served by offenders.
    II. Parole caused the release of many dangerous, unrehabilitated criminals into society.
    III. A suitable system for determining parole eligibility did not exist.
    The CORRECT answer is:

    A. I, II
    B. I, III
    C. II, III
    D. I, II, III

18. The *logical consequences* model, an emerging model in juvenile probation, is based on a number of assumptions. Which of the following is NOT one of these?

    A. It is not usually necessary to include serious punishments in a juvenile probation program; the emphasis should be on needs assessment and rehabilitation.
    B. Juvenile offenders have free will and should be held responsible for what they do.
    C. It is possible to develop effective relationships with juvenile probationers once they decide to take probation seriously.
    D. Youthful offenders will only modify their behavior when the cost of their behavior becomes too high.

19. Under the conventional model of caseload assignment, probation or parole officers are assigned to clients

    A. randomly
    B. according to the nature of the offense
    C. geographically
    D. according to the training of the officer

20. Approximately what percentage of inmates who enter parole supervision each year in the United States have committed violent offenses?

    A. 10   B. 25   C. 35   D. 45

21. The correctional model based on the concept of *just desserts* is the _____ model.

    A. penal
    B. justice
    C. presumptive
    D. medical

22. A parole officer may issue a warrant for a parolee's return to prison only after the warrant has been issued by the

    A. local law enforcement agency
    B. parole board
    C. local court
    D. corrections department

23. Which of the following is NOT an example of an intermittent sentence?
    An

    A. offender's location is electronically monitored
    B. offender must serve weekends in jail
    C. offender must spend specific weeknights in home confinement
    D. offender must adhere to a curfew

24. Which of the following is most commonly a criticism of halfway houses?
    They

    A. do not provide for the basic needs of clients
    B. tend to cost more than incarceration
    C. don't tend to support the long-term maintenance of client employment
    D. are not effective in preventing criminal behavio

25. Based on parole officers' experiences, which of the following factors is least likely to function as a predictor of a parolee's successful reintegration?

    A. Marital status
    B. Participation in academic or vocational programs
    C. Good prison behavior
    D. Prior problems with drug/alcohol abuse

KEY (CORRECT ANSWERS)

1. B
2. D
3. A
4. B
5. B

6. A
7. A
8. C
9. B
10. A

11. C
12. A
13. B
14. C
15. C

16. C
17. C
18. A
19. A
20. B

21. B
22. B
23. A
24. C
25. C

TEST 3

DIRECTIONS: Each question or incomplete statement is followed by several suggested answers or completions. Select the one that BEST answers the question or completes the statement. *PRINT THE LETTER OF THE CORRECT ANSWER IN THE SPACE AT THE RIGHT.*

1. What is the term for a document given to a prisoner as a result of accumulating good-time marks, which obligates the prisoner to remain under limited jurisdiction and supervision of local police?

    A. ROR
    B. Ticket-of-leave
    C. Conditional release
    D. Provisional certificate

    1.____

2. In contrast to other post-release correctional programs, work release programs emphasize

    A. responsibility for dependents
    B. community service
    C. the provision of shelter
    D. victim restitution

    2.____

3. The probation/parole officer work-role in which the offender seeks to instruct and assist offenders in dealing with problems as they arise is the _____ role.

    A. promoter   B. enabler   C. enforcer   D. broker

    3.____

4. In recent years, criticisms of probation and parole programs in the United States have included
    I. insufficient licensing mechanisms for officer certification
    I. PO training based on same military model used for police training
    II. lack of coordination with other criminal justice agencies
    III. selection procedures for officers based on physical attributes and security considerations

    The CORRECT answer is:

    A. I, III, IV
    B. II, III
    C. III, IV
    D. I, II, III, IV

    4.____

5. Which of the following was NOT a reason for the decline in the significance and influence of the rehabilitative model in United States corrections?

    A. Unacceptable levels of recidivism
    B. The rise of victims' rights movement
    C. Rising crime rates
    D. General dissension among corrections professionals

    5.____

6. The average length of time for an offender to spend on parole is about _____ months.

    A. 8   B. 19   C. 27   D. 38

    6.____

7. Judges often sentence low-risk offenders to incarceration with a strong warning that they be encouraged to apply for intensive probation supervision programs. This process is known as

    A. alternative sentencing
    B. backdooring
    C. screening
    D. stacking

8. Which of the following is a commonly perceived DISADVANTAGE associated with electronic monitoring?

    A. Studies show higher recidivism rates than standard probation
    B. More costly than standard monitoring procedures
    C. Those chosen for participation tend to be those who do not require monitoring anyway
    D. Does not accommodate special-needs clients

9. The primary distinguishing feature between probation and parole is that

    A. parole involves a clear instance of conviction
    B. parole involves indeterminate sentencing
    C. probation is granted or imposed as a sentence by a judge
    D. probation is a fixed-term situation

10. Among paroling agencies, the most desirable outcome measure for the effectiveness of a parole program is

    A. family stability
    B. new arrests
    C. the number of supervision terms completed
    D. the amount of restitution collected

11. What is the term for a parole board decision-making system that regards such decisions as a natural part of the criminal justice process, and in which fairness and equity predominate?

    A. Specialized caseloads systems
    B. Jurist value system
    C. Controller value system
    D. Regulator value system

12. Which of the following is most commonly used as an item in a paroling authority's release risk instruments?

    A. Drug use
    B. Number of prior convictions
    C. Total years incarcerated
    D. Number of parole revocations

13. Standard conditions of probation and parole typically include
    I. reporting a change of address
    II. remaining employed
    III. performing community service
    IV. not leaving the jurisdiction without permission

    The CORRECT answer is:

A. I, II B. I, III, IV
C. I, II, IV D. III, IV

14. Most state work release programs require that eligible candidates must have served at LEAST _____% of their incarcerative sentence.

   A. 10 B. 30 C. 50 D. 70

15. What is the term for the administratively authorized early release of an offender from custody?

   A. Abrogation B. Commutation
   C. Rescission D. Surrogation

16. In the traditional model of parole agency orientation, the emphasis is most often placed on

   A. the specialization of officers in certain kinds of problems
   B. offender change
   C. increased accountability for service availability
   D. even distribution of caseloads among officers

17. Each of the following is generally a difference between probationers and parolees in United States corrections EXCEPT

   A. the offenses of parolees are more serious
   B. parolees have been convicted
   C. parolees have been incarcerated for a portion of their sentences
   D. the conditions of probation are not as stringent

18. Which of the following statements about recidivism is generally TRUE?

   A. The greater the intensity of supervision, the less likely the recidivism
   B. The earlier offenders begin their careers, the more likely the recidivism
   C. The longer the time served in prison, the less likely the recidivism
   D. Violent offenders are more likely to recidivate than property offenders

19. The Federal Sentencing Reform Act of 1984

   A. encouraged the states' adoption of *three strikes* sentencing statutes
   B. established a mechanism for investigating charges of sentencing disparity
   C. provided federal judges and others with discretionary powers to provide alternative sentencing
   D. extended the death penalty to a number of drug crimes

20. Participants in day reporting programs should probably NOT include

   A. those with an established residence
   B. inmates within 6 months of release
   C. sex offenders
   D. those without an identified victim

21. Which of the following is most likely to be considered a latent function of parole?

   A. Integrating offenders into a structured community
   B. Separating offenders from the criminal element

C. Alleviating prison overcrowding
D. Preventing recidivism

22. Compared to routine court procedures related to fine assessment and payment, day-fine structures involve the advantage of
    I. fewer warrants for nonappearance at postsentence hearings
    II. greater victim satisfaction
    III. fewer court appearances
    IV. more extended terms of payment for larger fines
    The CORRECT answer is:

    A. I, II
    B. I, III, IV
    C. II, IV
    D. III, IV

23. The most important factor distinguishing between a *halfway in* and a *halfway out* house is

    A. whether the goal of the program is reintegration
    B. whether participants are probationers or parolees
    C. the variety of services available to participants
    D. the amount of time served by participating inmates

24. Most recidivists tend to

    A. be under correctional supervision when committing new offenses
    B. commit progressively more serious offenses
    C. be under 30 years of age
    D. be unemployed when committing new offenses

25. Approximately what percentage of adult prisoners being held in jails today are pretrial detainees?

    A. 10   B. 30   C. 50   D. 70

KEY (CORRECT ANSWERS)

1.	B	11.	B
2.	D	12.	D
3.	B	13.	C
4.	D	14.	A
5.	B	15.	B
6.	B	16.	D
7.	B	17.	B
8.	C	18.	B
9.	C	19.	C
10.	D	20.	C

21. C
22. B
23. B
24. C
25. C

EXAMINATION SECTION
TEST 1

DIRECTIONS: Each question or incomplete statement is followed by several suggested answers or completions. Select the one that BEST answers the question or completes the statement. *PRINT THE LETTER OF THE CORRECT ANSWER IN THE SPACE AT THE RIGHT.*

1. The institution of parole rests on the concepts of
    I.   retribution
    II. contract of consent
    III. custody
    IV. grace or privilege
   The CORRECT answer is:

   A. I, III
   B. II, IV
   C. II, III, IV
   D. I, II, III, IV

   1.____

2. _____ sentencing occurs when the court is required to impose an incarcerative sentence of a specified length, without the option for probation, suspended sentence, or immediate parole eligibility.

   A. Guidelines-based
   B. Mandatory
   C. Presumptive
   D. Determinate

   2.____

3. Each of the following is generally considered to be an advantage associated with community service as a form of corrections EXCEPT

   A. unambiguous punishment
   B. court benefit of sentencing alternatives
   C. community benefit of restitution
   D. reintegration of offenders in responsible, law-abiding roles

   3.____

4. Some electronic monitoring devices function by telephoning an offender at random hours to verify that he is where he is supposed to be. These are _____ devices.

   A. programmed contact
   B. vicarious monitoring
   C. random access
   D. continuous signaling

   4.____

5. Which of the following is the basic change strategy involved in the deterrence model of probation practice?

   A. Care and control
   B. Punishment
   C. Surveillance
   D. Threats

   5.____

6. Which of the following is NOT considered to be a goal common to all community corrections programs?

   A. Maintaining some degree of ostracism
   B. Facilitating offender reintegration
   C. Heightening offender accountability
   D. Fostering rehabilitation

   6.____

7. Which of the following court cases established the minimum due process requirements for offenders undergoing parole revocation proceedings?

   A. *In re Gault* (1967)
   B. *Mempa v. Rhay* (1967)
   C. *McKeiver v. Pennsylvania* (1970)
   D. *Morrissey v. Brewer* (1972)

8. The SFS/81 guidelines for parole release decisions include each of the following scoring items EXCEPT

   A. heroin/opiate dependence
   B. recent commitment-free period
   C. age at current offense/prior commitments
   D. employment history

9. Which of the following is/are a type of unconditional release?
   I. Mandatory parole
   II. Expiration
   III. Commutation
   IV. Parole board release

   The CORRECT answer is:

   A. I, III   B. I, IV   C. II, III   D. II, IV

10. Other than the requirement to obey all federal, state, and local laws, the condition of parole most often imposed by United States paroling authorities is that the offender

    A. meet family responsibilities and support dependents
    B. remain within the jurisdiction of the court and notify the officer of any change in residence
    C. maintain gainful employment
    D. report to the parole officer as directed and answer all reasonable inquiries

11. Which of the following was a ruling in the 1975 *Breed v. Jones* case?

    A. Deliberate indifference by prison authorities to serious medical disorders of prisoners violates the Eighth Amendment as *cruel and unusual punishment.*
    B. A juvenile may not be adjudicated as delinquent in juvenile courts and then tried as adults in criminal courts later on the same charges.
    C. A probationer is entitled to have court-appointed counsel at hearings concerning violations of the terms of probation.
    D. Female inmates must receive equal corrections programming.

12. A parole officer and an offender list a high number of supervision objectives in their parole plan. This generally indicates a

    A. lack of trust between the officer and the offender
    B. high emphasis on control for the officer
    C. high degree of centralized bureaucratic control
    D. high emphasis on assistance for the officer

13. When an offender is placed in prison for a brief period, primarily to give him a sense of prison life, and then released into the custody of a probation or parole officer, the offender has undergone

    A. role ambiguity
    B. mixed sentencing
    C. unconditional diversion
    D. shock probation

14. In juvenile corrections, the equivalent of a presentence investigation is the

    A. delinquency petition
    B. predispositional report
    C. detention hearing
    D. demand waiver

15. The significant problems in providing correctional treatment for white-collar offenders include
    I. not requiring job training
    II. their not being receptive to counseling
    III. their correctional term is typically too short to be influential
    IV. they are likely to come from an environment plagued by social problems
    The CORRECT answer is:

    A. I, II
    B. I, II, III
    C. I, III, IV
    D. II, III, IV

16. In the *numbers game* model of assignment for probation or parole officers,

    A. the total number of offender-clients is divided by the number of officers
    B. the number of cases assigned to an officer is proportional to his/her years of experience
    C. each officer tries to outperform the other by taking on an escalating number of clients
    D. the number of cases worked by an officer is constantly changing

17. Which of the following is LEAST likely to be a statutory element of a parole board's decision to grant parole release?

    A. Probability of recidivism
    B. Sufficiency of the parole plan
    C. Offense seriousness
    D. The conduct of the offender while in the correctional institution

18. A corrections department formulates a restitution program that emphasizes the offender's accountability and service to pay for damages inflicted on the victims, as well as to defray a portion of prosecution expenses.
    This program could be said to be following the _____ model.

    A. medical-reintegration
    B. financial-community service
    C. victim-offender mediation
    D. victim reparations

19. It is generally agreed among corrections professionals that the period of greatest vulnerability for formerly drug-dependent inmates who reenter the community is the _____ release.

    A. first six months following
    B. period beginning six months after
    C. first two years following
    D. period beginning one year after

20. The _____ value system is used by parole boards in early-release decision making in which the amount of time served is equated with the seriousness of the conviction offense.

    A. sanctioner   B. selective
    C. punitive   D. regulator

21. In the juvenile justice system, what is the equivalent of a formal charge?

    A. Disposition   B. Adjudication
    C. Intake   D. Petition

22. What is the term used to denote taking only the most qualified offenders for succeeding in rehabilitative programs?

    A. Skimming   B. Backdooring
    C. Creaming   D. Screening

23. Which of the following would be an element of a regular or differential scheme for juvenile parole supervision?

    A. 2 face-to-face contacts per month with parents
    B. 3 face-to-face contacts per month with placement staff
    C. 6 face-to-face contacts per month with youth alone
    D. 3 contacts with school officials

24. A _____ sentence has a different meaning from the others.

    A. mandatory   B. straight
    C. determinate   D. fixed

25. In evaluating a parole program's effectiveness in enforcing court-ordered sanctions, the most appropriate performance indicator would be

    A. number and type of arrests during supervision
    B. number of favorable discharges
    C. payment of restitution
    D. employment during supervision

KEY (CORRECT ANSWERS)

1. C
2. B
3. A
4. A
5. D

6. A
7. D
8. D
9. C
10. D

11. B
12. D
13. D
14. B
15. A

16. A
17. C
18. B
19. A
20. A

21. D
22. C
23. A
24. A
25. B

TEST 2

DIRECTIONS: Each question or incomplete statement is followed by several suggested answers or completions. Select the one that BEST answers the question or completes the statement. *PRINT THE LETTER OF THE CORRECT ANSWER IN THE SPACE AT THE RIGHT.*

1. The _____ value system is the term for a parole board decisipn-making system that is oriented toward the inmates' reactions to parole board decisions.

    A. regulator
    B. jurist value
    C. controller
    D. congregate

2. The reintegrative tasks of a probation department typically include
    I. assessing the willingness of the community to accept offender reintegration
    II. encouraging and conducting research designed to develop and improve reintegrative techniques for offenders
    III. providing information and recommendations to the courts that will assist in achieving dispositions favorable to reintegration
    IV. assessing the personal and social conditions of persons referred for probation services

    The CORRECT answer is:

    A. I, II
    B. II, III, IV
    C. III, IV
    D. I, III

3. According to the _____ philosophy of probation and parole management, the goal is to maximize the caseload while minimizing supervisory costs, time expenditures, and client criminality.

    A. conservationist
    B. cost/benefit
    C. due process
    D. economic

4. Which of the following is LEAST likely to be an effect of the growth of presumptive and determinate sentencing on inmate furlough programs?

    A. Impossibility of conforming to statutory prohibitions
    B. Decreased success rate
    C. Reductions in inmate incentives to abide by institutional rules
    D. Higher administrative costs

5. One approach to criminology is based on the assumption that human behavior is a product of biological, economic, psychological, and social factors, and that the scientific method can be used to establish the causes of an individual's behavior.
    This school of thought is known as the _____ school.

    A. determinist
    B. behaviorist
    C. positivist
    D. empirical

6. Which of the following is NOT typically a formal role expectation for a parole officer?

    A. Gathering information necessary for the parole board to make a parole decision
    B. To recommend, when necessary, an issue for a warrant returning a parolee to prison

C. Providing presentence reports
D. Insuring that parolees receive their due process rights during revocation hearings

7. Approximately what percentage of conditional inmate releases are mandatory in nature?

   A. 10   B. 33   C. 50   D. 66

8. In general, it is recommended that day reporting programs operate under each of the following conditions EXCEPT

   A. twice-weekly urinalysis
   B. notification of the police department in the offender's hometown
   C. control of the offender's daily itinerary
   D. performance of spot-checks of the offender's home

9. In the late 19th century, the state of California began to implement its first parole system. Which of the following were purposes of this adoption?
   I. Effecting rehabilitation among offenders
   II. Minimizing the use of clemency by governors
   III. Alleviating prison overcrowding
   IV. Correcting or modifying excessive prison sentences in relation to certain crimes

   The CORRECT answer is:

   A. I, III   B. I, II, III
   C. II, IV   D. II, III, IV

10. Corrections officers sometimes attempt to predict the future behavior of inmates based on past circumstances.
    This process is known as

    A. analogous foretoken   B. actuarial prediction
    C. anamnestic prediction   D. clinical prediction

11. The factor most likely to be associed with community-based corrections programs is

    A. state government funding
    B. affiliation with work release
    C. application of electronic monitoring
    D. some degree of home confinement

12. The United States Sentencing Commission's guidelines recommend that a defendant shall notify a parole officer within _____ hours of any change of residence or employment.

    A. 24   B. 48   C. 64   D. 72

13. The ability of a person to obtain compliance by the manipulation of symbolic rewards is known as _____ power.

    A. coercive   B. legitimate
    C. normative   D. administrative

14. Which of the following statements concerning judicial actions and probationer/parolee rights is TRUE?

    A. Judges may revoke a program or probation or parole and impose a new sentence that the offender must serve the remainder of the term in confinement.
    B. Defendants may not refuse probation of the court imposes it as a sentence.
    C. Probationers may not be obligated to pay supervision fees to defray program expenses, even if they are financially able to do so.
    D. Ordinarily, sentences of probation may be served simultaneously with sentences of incarceration.

15. The collective term for attempts to categorize the future behaviors of persons charged with or convicted of crimes is

    A. screening
    B. risk assessment
    C. augury
    D. needs assessment

16. What is the term for an action filed by a juvenile and his/her attorney to have a case in juvenile court transferred to the jurisdiction of criminal courts?

    A. Demand waiver
    B. Bench warrant
    C. Detainer warrant
    D. Delinquency petition

17. Correctional methods such as home incarceration and electronic monitoring are often referred to as

    A. community-based corrections
    B. intermediate punishments
    C. intermittent sentences
    D. diversions

18. Which of the following is considered to be a DISADVANTAGE associated with home confinement programs?
    It

    A. is not cost-effective
    B. focuses on offender surveillance
    C. is not responsive to local citizen needs
    D. has no perceivable social benefits

19. Among most corrections agencies, the most popular type of juvenile parole is

    A. determinate parole set by administrative agency
    B. indeterminate parole with a specified maximum and a discretionary minimum length of supervision
    C. indeterminate or purely discretionary parole
    D. presumptive minimum with discretionary extension of supervision for an indeterminate period

20. In the _____ model of supervision, the probation/parole officer focuses on helping offenders comply with the conditions of their release.

    A. justice
    B. casework

C. brokerage
D. community resource management

21. Each of the following is a commonly-encountered problem in providing treatment for street offenders EXCEPT they

   A. see no need for rehabilitation
   B. are more likely to commit violent crimes than other types of offenses
   C. tend to come from problem environments
   D. often belong to prison gangs or a subculture that disapproves of participation in treatment

22. The numerical score used by parole boards and agencies to forecast an offender's risk to the public and future dangerousness is known as a(n) _____ score.

   A. public risk   B. offense probability
   C. salient factor   D. clearance

23. According to most research, the act of exiting from crime appears to depend on a set of interrelated processes.
   Which of the following is NOT typically one of these?

   A. Developing an escalating fear of punishment
   B. Having successful community experiences
   C. Maturing out of crime
   D. Developing internal resources

24. *Cleared by arrest* is a term used by the FBI in its UNIFORM CRIME REPORTS to indicate that someone has been

   A. arrested and charged for a reported crime
   B. arrested for a reported crime
   C. charged for a crime and prosecution has been initiated
   D. arrested and confessed to a reported crime

25. The typical period of incarceration for an offender undergoing shock probation is _____ days.

   A. 10-30   B. 15-60   C. 30-120   D. 120-240

KEY (CORRECT ANSWERS)

1.	A	11.	B
2.	B	12.	D
3.	D	13.	C
4.	B	14.	A
5.	C	15.	B
6.	C	16.	A
7.	B	17.	B
8.	C	18.	B
9.	C	19.	C
10.	C	20.	A

21. B
22. C
23. A
24. B
25. C

TEST 3

DIRECTIONS: Each question or incomplete statement is followed by several suggested answers or completions. Select the one that BEST answers the question or completes the statement. *PRINT THE LETTER OF THE CORRECT ANSWER IN THE SPACE AT THE RIGHT.*

1. In the initial stages of parole supervision, a strong attachment tends to exist between the   1.____

    A. bureaucracy and the community
    B. parolee and the officer
    C. officer and the bureaucracy
    D. parolee and the bureaucracy

2. Which of the following statements about recidivism is generally TRUE?   2.____

    A. Females are more likely than males to recidivate.
    B. Parolees who recidivate tend to do so for crimes different from the ones for which they were originally imprisoned.
    C. Recidivism decreases as participation in programs such as furlough, study release, and other prerelease programs increase.
    D. The number of prior arrests does not correlate strongly with recidivism.

3. What is the term for a prosecutor-initiated charge against a criminal defendant?   3.____

    A. Information   B. Imputation
    C. Indictment   D. Billing

4. Each of the following elements is considered to be essential for the success of community-corrections programs EXCEPT   4.____

    A. use of a specific formula for fund allocation
    B. financial subsidies provided to local government and community agencies
    C. targeting offenders who are not prison- or jail-bound
    D. local advisory boards in each community

5. Which of the following statements about potential parolees who are released into home confinement programs is TRUE? They   5.____

    A. have troubled institutional records
    B. are more likely to have drug or alcohol dependencies
    C. have stable home environments
    D. are generally younger than other potential parolees

6. Which of the following items of federal legislation authorizes the allocation of a certain amount of work releasee wages for restitution and a general victim compensation fund?   6.____

    A. Victim and Witness Protection Act of 1982
    B. Victims of Crime Act of 1984
    C. Victims of Child Abuse Act of 1990
    D. Crime Control Act of 1994

25

7. Which of the following was a ruling in the 1984 *Schall v. Martin* case?

    A. Parole revocation hearings must consist of two stages: determination of probable cause that a violation has occurred, and punishment.
    B. Courts have a right to order the pretrial detention of a juvenile deemed to be dangerous.
    C. Juveniles are not entitled to a jury as a matter of course.
    D. The state takes precedence over the family in deciding the best interests of children.

8. What is the term for rehabilitative treatment that focuses on how a person interacts with others, especially in situations that reveal personal problems?

    A. Unit management
    B. Transactional analysis
    C. Behavioral reintegration
    D. Utilitarianism

9. In jurisdictions where the *parole as grace* concept operates, parole officers are generally granted which of the following powers?
The
    I. search of a parolee's living quarters without warning or warrant
    II. suspension of parole pending a board hearing
    III. arrest of a parolee for suspected violations without the possibility of bail
    IV. use of incriminating statements made by a parolee during noncustodial questioning

    The CORRECT answer is:

    A. I only
    B. I, II, III
    C. II only
    D. II, III, IV

10. The convicted offender's version of events leading to the conviction offense, often included in records relating to a specific offense, is known as the

    A. offense sequential
    B. impact statement
    C. incident report
    D. sentencing memorandum

11. One philosophy of parole is that the parolee is still under the supervision of the parole authorities or the prison, and that his constitutional rights are limited. This is the _____ theory.

    A. contract
    B. continuing custody
    C. degree of justice
    D. medical

12. For most of the period between 1900 and 1960, the principle of _____ was of primary importance in the operation of United States corrections.

    A. isolation
    B. rehabilitation
    C. retribution
    D. deterrence

13. What is the term for a charge issued by a grand jury upon its own authority against a specific criminal defendant?

    A. Charge bill
    B. Arraignment
    C. Conferral
    D. Presentment

14. What is the term for a notice of criminal charges or unserved sentences pending against a prisoner in the same or other jurisdictions?

    A. Presentment
    B. Demand waiver
    C. Detainer warrant
    D. Detention hearing

15. Though the functions of parole boards often vary from state to state, most share some common functions. These include
    I. evaluating juveniles to determine their eligibility for release from detention
    II. providing investigative and supervisory services to smaller jurisdictions within the state
    III. review pardons and executive clemency decisions made by governors
    IV. commuting death penalties or granting reprieves

    The CORRECT answer is:

    A. I, II
    B. I, III
    C. II, III, IV
    D. I, II, III, IV

16. The tendency for social control mechanisms to encompass a larger (or different) population than originally intended is known as

    A. mission creep
    B. outlawry
    C. role conflict
    D. net widening

17. Nationwide, which of an offender's due process rights is least likely to be provided at a revocation hearing?

    A. Written statement of reasons for the revocation decision
    B. Written notice of alleged violation
    C. Representation by counsel
    D. Opportunity to confront and cross-examine witnesses

18. The legal term applicable to juveniles who have not attained the age of majority (in most states, 18) is

    A. slip
    B. infant
    C. adolescent
    D. minor

19. What is the term for a parole board decision-making system that is concerned with appealing to the public interests and seeing that community expectations are met? _____ value system.

    A. Citizen
    B. Jurist
    C. Treater
    D. Regulator

20. Which of the following is a form of probation imposed before a plea of guilt that can result in a dismissal of the charges?

    A. Nominal disposition
    B. Presentment
    C. Pretrial diversion
    D. Deferred adjudication

21. Which of the following statements about presumptive sentencing is FALSE? It

    A. usually results in a universal sentence for particular crimes
    B. is designed to reduce sentencing disparities associated with race, gender, ethnicity, or socio-economic status

C. specifies ranges of time for different degrees of offense seriousness
D. takes an offender's prior record into account

22. The fear aroused by the construction of halfway houses for parolees is often referred to as the fear of 22.___

    A. community degeneration
    B. criminal contamination
    C. crimogenesis
    D. assured recidivism

23. The primary manifest goal of community-based corrections is 23.___

    A. crime control
    B. restitution
    C. deterrence
    D. societal reintegration

24. The purpose of a preliminary hearing in criminal proceedings is to 24.___

    A. determine if a person charged with a crime should be held for trial
    B. examine a defendant's prior criminal history
    C. present evidence relating to the defendant's character
    D. discuss the possibility of intermediate punishment for a crime

25. On average, parole accounts for about _____% of all correctional time served for United States offenders in all categories. 25.___

    A. 20
    B. 40
    C. 60
    D. 80

KEY (CORRECT ANSWERS)

1.	C	11.	B
2.	C	12.	B
3.	A	13.	D
4.	C	14.	C
5.	C	15.	D
6.	B	16.	D
7.	B	17.	C
8.	B	18.	B
9.	B	19.	A
10.	D	20.	C

21. A
22. B
23. D
24. A
25. B

EXAMINATION SECTION
TEST 1

DIRECTIONS: Each question or incomplete statement is followed by several suggested answers or completions. Select the one that BEST answers the question or completes the statement. *PRINT THE LETTER OF THE CORRECT ANSWER IN THE SPACE AT THE RIGHT.*

1. Which of the following was originally a device of preventive justice that obliged persons suspected of future misbehavior to stipulate with and give full assurance to the court and the public that the apprehended offense would not occur?

    A. Parole
    B. Bail
    C. Recognizance
    D. Probation

    1.____

2. Which of the following statements about parolee rights and parole board actions is FALSE?

    A. Inmates who become eligible for parole are not automatically entitled to parole.
    B. If a parole board imposes a special condition of parole, it may not be challenged on the grounds of the Fifth Amendment right against self-incrimination.
    C. Inmates who have been paroled and subsequently commit a violent act while on parole may have parole revoked and be returned to prison, regardless of trial or conviction for the new crime.
    D. Parole boards must recognize minimum-sentence provisions from sentencing judges when considering an inmate's parole eligibility.

    2.____

3. Which of the following is an administrative procedure designed to furnish personal background information to a bonding company and law enforcement officials?

    A. Booking
    B. Classification
    C. Arraignment
    D. Bailment

    3.____

4. Criminologists report that along the scale of age, offenders typically cease criminal activity at two points. These are the

    A. early teens and early 60s
    B. late teens and mid-30s
    C. late teens and late 40s
    D. late 20s and mid-50s

    4.____

5. The legal term for a period of proving a trial or foregiveness is

    A. novitio   B. assai   C. catechism   D. probatio

    5.____

6. Some corrections reformists argue that the privatization of community-based programs would improve their effectiveness. Which of the following is NOT a reason given for this?

    A. Greater incentive to make rehabilitation work
    B. Greater accountability
    C. Consolidation of program control with professional corrections personnel
    D. Promotion of new ideas and strategies for treatment

    6.____

7. In _____ sentencing, an inmate's final release date is decided by the parole board.

    7.____

A. determinate
B. indeterminate
C. presumptive
D. guidelines-based

8. What is the commonly used term for the federal statute that permits probationers, parolees, and inmates of prisons and jails to challenge the fact, length, and conditions of their confinement or placement in particular facilities or programs?

A. *Blue Sky* laws
B. Due process laws
C. *Habeas corpus* statute
D. The exclusionary rule

9. Over the last two decades or so, federal and state legislation concerning corrections has generally produced each of the following results EXCEPT to

A. broadening parole board authority for making early prisoner release decisions
B. limiting the discretionary sentencing power of judges
C. decrease the likelihood of sentence disparities
D. increase prisoner release predictability and the certainty of incarceration

10. Generally, in order to qualify for electronic monitoring programs, candidates must

A. seek and maintain employment
B. be assessed as high-risk offenders
C. have special care requirements that can only be fulfilled by family members
D. have no more than 180 days to serve in jail

11. What is the term for a specific criminal act involving one or more victims?

A. Felony
B. Offense
C. Index crime
D. Incident

12. Approximately what percentage of a probation or parole officer's working time is typically made available for client supervision?

A. 10   B. 30   C. 50   D. 70

13. Of the following, inmates who have committed _____ crimes are on average most likely to successfully complete a term of parole supervision.

A. public order
B. drug
C. violent
D. property

14. The primary distinguishing factor between standard and intensive supervision probation programs is the

A. amount of consultative services offered
B. strictness of punitive conditions
C. amount of face-to-face contact
D. number of agency personnel assigned to the case

15. Which of the following statements are TRUE of the day fine process?
   I. The value of each day-fine unit is calculated according to a percentage of the offender's daily income
   II. The seriousness of the offense is determined subjectively by an appointed board
   III. The number of day-fine units is calculated according to offense severity

The CORRECT answer is:

A. I only   B. I, III   C. II, III   D. III only

16. For most of the period between 1820 and 1900, the prevailing philosophy operating in most United States corrections was that of

    A. isolation
    B. rehabilitation
    C. retribution
    D. deterrence

17. Which of the following is NOT an advantage associated with objective parole criteria?

    A. The use of composite group scores to predict parole success
    B. Greater discretionary power granted to parole boards
    C. Knowledge of presumptive release dates within several months of incarceration
    D. Time ranges for discharge are decided using fixed scoring systems

18. What type of electronic monitoring device is most useful for monitoring multiple clients simultaneously?

    A. Call-forwarding transmitter
    B. Cellular telephone device
    C. Programmed contact device
    D. Continuous signaling transmitter

19. The primary purpose of most prerelease programs is to

    A. provide a future parolee with skills or education that will facilitate reintegration
    B. evaluate the probability of a parolee's rehabilitation
    C. determine the likelihood of recidivism
    D. make reintegration a gradual process for future parolees

20. Which of the following is likely to be a special, rather than standard, condition of probation or parole?

    A. Notifying officer before applying for a marriage license
    B. Avoiding association with known or suspected criminals
    C. Prohibition against the possession of a firearm
    D. Finding and maintaining legitimate employment

21. What is the term for the official halting or suspension of legal proceedings against a defendant after a recorded justice system entry usually followed by a referral for treatment?

    A. Diversion
    B. Rehabilitation
    C. Disposition
    D. Commutation

22. The commonly used term for any probation or parole officer who works with probationers or parolees as clients is

    A. corrector
    B. caseworker
    C. chancery
    D. broker

23. What is the legal term for the principle that punishment should correspond in degree and kind with the offense?

    A. Lex talionis
    B. Parens patriae
    C. Damnum absque injuria
    D. Respondeat superior

24. Which of the following is regarded as *symbolic* restitution?

    A. Day-fine programs
    B. Victim-offender mediation
    C. Victim reparations
    D. Community service

25. A classification system is a traditional means used by probation/parole agencies to separate offenders according to characteristics related to the

    A. background of the offenders
    B. type of correctional treatments applied to the offenders in the past
    C. nature and seriousness of the offenses
    D. relative amount of correctional treatment undergone by the offenders

---

KEY (CORRECT ANSWERS)

1.	C	11.	D
2.	D	12.	B
3.	A	13.	A
4.	B	14.	C
5.	D	15.	B
6.	C	16.	D
7.	B	17.	B
8.	C	18.	B
9.	A	19.	D
10.	A	20.	C

21. A
22. B
23. A
24. D
25. C

TEST 2

DIRECTIONS: Each question or incomplete statement is followed by several suggested answers or completions. Select the one that BEST answers the question or completes the statement. *PRINT THE LETTER OF THE CORRECT ANSWER IN THE SPACE AT THE RIGHT.*

1. Among paroling agencies, the LEAST desirable outcome measure for the effectiveness of a parole program is

    A. alcohol and drug test results
    B. technical violations
    C. number of offenders employed
    D. recidivism

    1.____

2. By the year _____, every state had adopted some form of a parole system.

    A. 1899 B. 1929 C. 1944 D. 1965

    2.____

3. In some programs, regardless of what a parole officer might think is best, he or she may be compelled to collect a supervision fee from an indigent client. This is an example of

    A. burnout   B. role ambiguity
    C. transactional discord D. role conflict

    3.____

4. An offender who is considered unlikely to commit future crimes is described as

    A. status   B. situational
    C. incidental   D. rehabilitated

    4.____

5. In the juvenile justice system, what is the equivalent of a trial?

    A. Disposition   B. Adjudication
    C. Diversion   D. Petition

    5.____

6. Which of the following is a highly structured nonresidential correction program that uses supervision, sanctions, and services coordinated from a central location?

    A. Halfway house   B. Community work center
    C. Day reporting center   D. Halfway out-house

    6.____

7. Which of the following is a manifest function of parole?

    A. Compensating for sentence disparities
    B. Offender reintegration
    C. Decreasing prison and jail overcrowding
    D. Public safety and protection

    7.____

8. In certain criminal cases that are viewed as not requiring an immediate sentence, an indictment may be held in abeyance without either dismissal or final judgment. This procedure is known as

    A. dormancy   B. intercession
    C. dissolution   D. filing

    8.____

9. One perceived drawback to the recent movement toward the *professionalization* of careers in probation and parole is that it

   A. is often equated with formal academic training rather than the acquisition of practical skills
   B. is more likely to attract people who are less able to deal with inmates on an interpersonal level
   C. has not yet resulted in a clear set of universal standards for professional contact
   D. makes it more difficult and costly for people to enter the field

10. What term describes the parole board decision-making system that emphasizes rehabilitation and early-release decisions made on the basis of the offender's needs? _____ value system.

    A. Regulator
    B. Jurist
    C. Controller
    D. Treater

11. The functions of most halfway houses include
    I. provisions of food and shelter
    II. rehabilitation and reintegration
    III. client-specific treatments
    IV. provision of victim or community restitution

    The CORRECT answer is:

    A. I, II, III
    B. II only
    C. II, III, IV
    D. IV only

12. The act of removing a conviction from official records is accomplished through a(n)

    A. discretionary waiver
    B. nominal disposition
    C. expungement order
    D. predisposition report

13. Each of the following is considered to be a function of a community corrections program EXCEPT

    A. making decisions about program enrollment
    B. ensuring public safety
    C. networking with other community agencies and businesses
    D. individual and group counseling

14. The most common organizational model for juvenile paroling authorities is the _____ model.

    A. institutional
    B. consolidation
    C. regulatory
    D. autonomous

15. What is the term for the constitutional guarantee that no agent or instrument of government will use any procedures to arrest, prosecute, try, or punish any person other than those procedures prescribed by law?

    A. Burden of proof
    B. Habeas corpus
    C. Corpus delecti
    D. Due process

16. The majority of parole board decisions made today involve those who have committed _____ offenses.

    A. public order
    B. drug
    C. property
    D. violent

17. When a defendant enters a guilty plea with the expectation of receiving a more lenient sentence, he or she engages in

    A. intake screening
    B. determinate sentencing
    C. implicit plea bargaining
    D. preventive arraignment

18. A corrections department formulates a restitution program which focuses on compensating victims directly for their offenses. This program could be described as following the _____ model.

    A. victim reparations
    B. victim-offender mediation
    C. victim reconciliation
    D. financial-community service

19. The main difference between conditional release and parole release is that

    A. conditional release is largely a response to institutional overcrowding
    B. inmates are selected according to *good time*
    C. conditional release is established by statute
    D. there is no discretion involved in conditional release

20. Of the parolees who are returned to state prison for technical violations, the highest number of them

    A. leave the jurisdiction without permission
    B. are arrested on a new charge
    C. fail a drug test
    D. fail to report to the parole officer

21. The Federal Victim and Witness Protection Act of 1982 was designed to

    A. create the Bureau of Justice Statistics
    B. require offenders to provide restitution to victims
    C. encourage the provision of alternate sentencing by federal judges and others
    D. increase the severity of sentencing for drug-related cases

22. In evaluating a parole program's effectiveness in protecting the community, the most appropriate performance indicator would be

    A. number of times attending treatment/work programming
    B. number of absconders during supervision
    C. extent of victim satisfaction with service and department
    D. timeliness of revocation and termination hearings

23. An interpersonal situation in which the likelihood of acquiring criminal behaviors is enhanced – such as in the view of many a prison – is described as a(n) _____ environment.

    A. crimogenic
    B. regressive
    C. apostatic
    D. recidivistic

24. The primary complaint lodged against work release programs by their participants tends to be that

    A. the pay is too low for the support of themselves and their families
    B. the strict supervision does not permit the assumption of adequate responsibility
    C. they are not accorded the same rights as members of labor organizations
    D. the jobs available to them do not require skills that are useful in the real world

25. Each of the following is generally considered to be a negative feature of indeterminate sentencing in relation to parole EXCEPT it

    A. can be abused to punish people with unpopular political beliefs
    B. applies therapy indiscriminately
    C. prevents correctional authorities from being forced to release an offender who is clearly not ready for reintegration
    D. is used primarily as a means of inmate control

KEY (CORRECT ANSWERS)

1.	D		11.	A
2.	C		12.	C
3.	D		13.	A
4.	B		14.	A
5.	B		15.	D
6.	C		16.	C
7.	B		17.	C
8.	D		18.	A
9.	A		19.	D
10.	D		20.	B

21. B
22. B
23. A
24. D
25. C

TEST 3

DIRECTIONS: Each question or incomplete statement is followed by several suggested answers or completions. Select the one that BEST answers the question or completes the statement. *PRINT THE LETTER OF THE CORRECT ANSWER IN THE SPACE AT THE RIGHT.*

1. In the justice model of probation practice, the most important role of a probation officer is to

    A. strengthen offender self-esteem
    B. supervise offenders
    C. police offender activities
    D. enforce probation rules

2. What is another term for the *civil disabilities* that follow a conviction and are not directly imposed by the sentencing court – such as loss of the right to vote, serve on a jury, or own a firearm?

    A. Collateral consequences   B. Custodial reproach
    C. Residual punishment   D. Associated correction

3. Which of the following is LEAST likely to be a source of stress for parole officers?

    A. Excessive paperwork
    B. Lack of collegial consortium
    C. High risk and liability exposure
    D. Role ambiguity

4. What is the general term used to describe programs and services such as halfway houses, psychological counseling services, employment assistance, and community-based correctional agencies?

    A. Diversion   B. Releases
    C. Deterrents   D. Aftercare

5. To a director or supervisor of a parole department, which of the following officer responsibilities would tend to take precedence over all others?

    A. One-on-one contact with and supervision of client
    B. Timely completion of reports to the court
    C. Insuring that clients know their due process rights during revocation hearings
    D. Location and referral of adequate client services

6. In the period from about 1985 to 1995, the parolee population in the United States grew by about _____%.

    A. 35   B. 50   C. 70   D. 100

7. Which of the following is most commonly used as an item in a paroling authority's release risk instruments?

    A. Prison infractions   B. Current crime involving violence
    C. Age at first incarceration   D. Length of current term

8. Which of the following is a theory of criminal behavior stressing the priority, duration, frequency, and intensity of interactions with other criminals?

    A. Deterrence
    B. Medical model
    C. Differential association
    D. Crimogenesis

9. Which of the following statements about recidivism is generally FALSE?

    A. Parolees tend to have higher recidivism rates than probationers.
    B. Shock incarceration has no influence on recidivism.
    C. Drug abuse and recidivism are not related.
    D. First-offenders tend to commit more violent crimes than chronic offenders.

10. Which of the following Supreme Court cases was the first to apply the *habeas corpus* rule to the actions of parole boards?

    A. *Jones v. Cunningham* (1963)
    B. *Mempa v. Rhay* (1967)
    C. *Morrissey v. Brewer* (1972)
    D. *Gagnon v. Soarpelli* (1973)

11. The process of predicting the future behavior of offenders based on a correctional professional's expert training and work is known as

    A. clinical prediction
    B. actuarial prediction
    C. anamnestic prediction
    D. risk analysis

12. Which of the following issues involved in the parole revocation process has thus far NOT been addressed by the United States Supreme Court?
    The

    A. cancellation of provisional release
    B. due process rights of offenders released under pre-parole
    C. right to appeal revocation
    D. right to counsel during a parole revocation hearing

13. Each of the following is a guideline typically used to direct the prisoner classification systems used by most modern correctional organizations EXCEPT

    A. the process must be applied uniformly among similarly situated inmates
    B. the system must provide for decentralized, inter-agency control over the process
    C. all inmates should be placed in the lowest custody level consistent with public safety
    D. inmates should be classified on the basis of objective information and criteria

14. The Supreme Court case which established a parole officer's right to search a client's residence was

    A. *Moody v. Daggett* (1976)
    B. *United States v. Addonizio* (1979)
    C. *Martinez v. California* (1987)
    D. *Griffin v. Wisconsin* (1987)

15. The primary purpose of structured discretion in both sentencing and parole decisions is to 15.____
    A. eliminate sentencing disparity
    B. standardize and create greater fairness in decisions
    C. emphasize the seriousness of violent crimes over others
    D. impose the maximum allowable sentence on serious offenders

16. Which of the following would be an element of an intensive scheme for juvenile parole supervision? 16.____
    A. 6 face-to-face contacts per month with youth alone
    B. 1 contact with school officials
    C. 1 face-to-face contact per month with parents
    D. 4 contacts with agency officials

17. In deferred adjudication, 17.____
    A. a defendant agrees to incarceration without a trial
    B. there is no formal finding of guilt
    C. there is a reduction in the offender's prison sentence
    D. an offender is not required to enter a plea

18. Which of the following forms of intervention has generally proven to be LEAST effective in the treatment of street offenders? 18.____
    A. Service-oriented programs
    B. Self-help
    C. Psychotherapy
    D. Skill development

19. Which of the following is NOT a widely recognized benefit of restitution as an intermediate sanction? 19.____
    A. Integrating the rehabilitative and punitive purposes of the criminal law
    B. Reducing demands on the criminal justice system
    C. Reducing the likelihood of sentence disparity
    D. Reduction in the perceived need for vengeance or vigilantism

20. Sometimes an officer's work-role is oriented so that he functions as a referral service and supplies an offender/client with contacts and agencies that provide services. This role is described as a(n) 20.____
    A. agent   B. enabler   C. broker   D. enforcer

21. The first use of work release as a correctional program in the United States occurred in 21.____
    A. 1832, in Massachusetts   B. 1865, in Mississippi
    C. 1906, in Vermont   D. 1942, in Idaho

22. A correctional institution that emphasizes security, discipline, and order is conforming to the _____ model of corrections. 22.____
    A. institutional   B. coercive
    C. custodial   D. medical

23. In the program model of parole agency orientation, the emphasis is most often placed on   23.____

    A. the specialization of officers in certain kinds of problems
    B. offender change
    C. increased accountability for service availability
    D. even distribution of caseloads among officers

24. What is the term for the finding by a grand jury that insufficient probable cause exists to   24.____
    proceed against one or more criminal defendants?

    A. Deficiency   B. No contest
    C. Dismissal   D. No true bill

25. In which of the following organizational models are parole decisions made by a central   25.____
    authority that has independent powers, but that is organizationally situated in the overall
    department of corrections?

    A. Consolidation   B. Autonomous
    C. Hierarchical   D. Incorporated

KEY (CORRECT ANSWERS)

1. C		11. A
2. A		12. C
3. B		13. B
4. D		14. D
5. B		15. B
6. D		16. A
7. B		17. B
8. C		18. C
9. A		19. C
10. A		20. C

21. C
22. C
23. A
24. D
25. A

CORRECTION SCIENCE

EXAMINATION SECTION
TEST 1

DIRECTIONS: Each question or incomplete statement is followed by several suggested answers or completions. Select the one that BEST answers the question or completes the statement. *PRINT THE LETTER OF THE CORRECT ANSWER IN THE SPACE AT THE RIGHT.*

1. The one of the following techniques that would NOT be helpful in a correctional program to raise the achievement level of school dropouts is to

    A. praise all work even if it is not merited
    B. encourage recognition by the peer group
    C. use money as the general reinforcer when appropriate
    D. provide programmed instruction

    1.____

2. Test validity is BEST described as

    A. the extent to which a test measures what it was designed to measure
    B. an index of reliability determined by correlating the scores of individuals on one form of a test with their scores on another form
    C. the degree to which a test measures anything consistently
    D. a mathematical index of the extent to which examinees believe an examination to be an appropriate testing instrument

    2.____

3. The one of the following which is NOT characteristic of traditional learning methods such as lectures, textbooks, films, television, records, and tapes is that

    A. the learner tends to be passive
    B. the learner may not get deeply involved in the learning process
    C. these methods prove invariably dull
    D. these methods are well adapted to the learning of new concepts

    3.____

4. The one of the following which would be MOST relevant to a decision concerning whether a particular occupation should be included in a vocational training program is the

    A. number of people currently employed in the occupation
    B. growth rate of the occupation in the recent past
    C. projected average annual openings in the occupation
    D. job turnover rate in an occupation through death or retirement

    4.____

5. Following are three statements about the use of correspondence courses for inmates:
    I. Practical courses such as agriculture, but not cultural courses, are adaptable to correspondence courses.
    II. Correspondence courses provide material for advanced courses in which too few inmates are interested to justify the organization of classes.
    III. One drawback of offering correspondence courses to inmates is that these students often do not make a proper selection of courses.

    Which one of the following *correctly* classifies the above statements?

    5.____

A. I and II are generally correct, but III is not.
B. II and III are generally correct, but I is not.
C. I is generally correct, but II and III are not.
D. II is generally correct, but I and III are not.

6. The one of the following which is of LEAST value in assessing the effectiveness of a training program for staff is

   A. change in the staff's knowledge
   B. the staff's feelings about the value of the program
   C. changes in the staff's attitudes or values
   D. the degree of success with clients by staff after they have completed the program

7. The one of the following which would be the MOST important factor in insuring that the participants successfully complete a training program is to

   A. increase the time allowed for training
   B. carefully select the trainees
   C. be sure that the material used in the course is readily available to the participants
   D. select instructors who are familiar with the material

8. Which of the following is a CORRECT statement regarding any significant proposed change in correctional practices such as the introduction of work-release programs?

   A. Costs of an innovation must be equal to or less than those of the present system.
   B. Recidivism is a minor factor when planning changes in correctional programs.
   C. Evidence must be provided that public protection is not diminished by the innovation.
   D. A change affecting the entire state system must be reviewed by the federal government.

9. The one of the following statements concerning the characteristics of offenders which is CORRECT is that offenders

   A. are seldom educationally handicapped
   B. tend to have stable work records
   C. usually have little self-esteem
   D. usually have a vocational skill

10. The one of the following that would be MOST helpful to an offender prior to his parole to prepare him to reenter the community is

    A. attendance at prerelease classes in penitentiaries
    B. prerelease visits by parole officers to the offender in the institution
    C. assignment to half-way houses for a period of time prior to release
    D. prerelease visits by parole officers to the family of the offender

11. The selection of a vocational skill to be taught in a training course should be made carefully.
    Of the following, the MOST important factor to consider when making the selection is the

    A. inherent interest of the program's content
    B. simplicity of the skill to be taught

C. attitude of society toward the institution
D. need for the skill in the community

12. The one of the following which is LEAST likely to be an element of a correctional training program based upon a behavior modification approach is

   A. specifying the desired final performance level
   B. holding a meeting between trainer and trainee to plan an individual program
   C. providing reinforcement of desired behaviors
   D. including factors to motivate the trainee

13. Of all the programs for misdemeanants, the LARGEST number of *innovative* efforts are being made for those dealing with

   A. domestic problems
   B. alcoholism
   C. juvenile delinquency
   D. gambling

14. Of the following, the LEAST important factor in motivating inmates of limited educational background to complete their high school education is the

   A. use of short, attainable, and measurable educational segments
   B. possibility of obtaining a high school'equivalency instead of obtaining a formal diploma
   C. substantial interpersonal relationship between the teacher and the student
   D. reinforcement of learning through recognition

15. There are several advantages in using televised videotape as a means of instruction. Which of the following is NOT an advantage of this method of teaching?

   A. A great number of viewers, spread over a large geographical area, can be reached.
   B. A variety of instructional materials can be integrated within a single lesson.
   C. It is a completely one-way process with the instructor separated from the students.
   D. The information and instruction, on tape, is available for replay whenever desired.

16. Which of the following statements concerning educational programs in correctional institutions is CORRECT?

   A. The costs of educational programming in the correctional setting are generally higher than in the regular educational systems.
   B. The subjects taught in correctional education programs are generally highly innovative.
   C. The status and priority established for institutional education is commensurate with today's demand for such education.
   D. Inmate teachers have rarely been used in educational programs in correctional institutions.

17. Assume that the goal of one of your training sessions for correctional staff is to make the staff aware of how it feels to be confined in a correctional institution. The training technique BEST suited to attain this goal is

   A. reading relevant literature
   B. role playing
   C. panel discussion
   D. group discussion

18. Following are three statements concerning programmed-learning textbooks:
    I. The subject matter is arranged logically and in small steps.
    II. The texts are structured so as to demand less concentration than that required for regular methods of instruction.
    III. If the learner has given an incorrect answer, he is immediately made aware of it so that he may correct it before proceeding with the lesson.
    Which of the following CORRECTLY classifies the above statements?

    A. I, II and III are correct.
    B. I and II are correct, but III is not.
    C. I and III are correct, but II is not.
    D. II and III are correct, but I is not.

19. For management by objectives to be successful, all of the following conditions must be fulfilled EXCEPT

    A. continuous feedback on managerial performance
    B. constant supervision of employees by supervisors
    C. an intensive training program preceding organizational implementation
    D. superior-subordinate relationships characterized by a high degree of cooperation and mutual respect

20. Which of the following types of programs is LEAST appropriate in a correctional institution? A(n)

    A. religious program
    B. recreational program
    C. individual counseling program
    D. methadone maintenance program

KEY (CORRECT ANSWERS)

1. A
2. A
3. C
4. C
5. B

6. B
7. B
8. C
9. C
10. C

11. D
12. B
13. B
14. B
15. C

16. A
17. B
18. C
19. B
20. D

TEST 2

DIRECTIONS: Each question or incomplete statement is followed by several suggested answers or completions. Select the one that BEST answers the question or completes the statement. *PRINT THE LETTER OF THE CORRECT ANSWER IN THE SPACE AT THE RIGHT.*

1. In a modern "information system," there are two main categories: "standard information," consisting of the data required for operational control, and "demand information," consisting of data which, although not needed regularly or under normal circumstances, must be available when required. Following are four types of data:
   I. Daily count at a prison
   II. Number of correctional officers who call in sick each day
   III. Number of prisoners eligible for release within the next six months in certain categories of offenses
   IV. Average number of paroles granted per year

   Which of the following CORRECTLY categorizes the above types of data into those which are "standard" and those which are "demand" items?

   A. I and II are standard, but III and IV are demand.
   B. I and III are standard, but II and IV are demand.
   C. III is standard, but I, II and IV are demand.
   D. II is standard, but I, III and IV are demand.

2. The *basis* purpose of a detention home for accused juvenile delinquents should be to

   A. serve as a shelter for dependent or neglected children who are temporarily without a home or parental supervision
   B. hold delinquent youngsters pending a court hearing or transfer to another jurisdiction or program
   C. act as a rehabilitative institution following adjudication
   D. act as a rehabilitation institution prior to adjudication

3. The *majority* of prisoners in jails in the United States are incarcerated because

   A. they are a serious threat to themselves and society
   B. they are too poor to get legal assistance
   C. it would cost the community more if they were released and committed offenses
   D. they are too poor to furnish bail pending trial

4. In an effort to assist defendants in obtaining legal counsel, the courts rely MOST heavily on

   A. the National Association for the Advancement of Colored People
   B. bar associations
   C. lawyers' guilds
   D. legal aid and public defender groups

5. All of the following are characteristics of minimum security prisons EXCEPT

   A. inmates work under general or intermittent supervision
   B. they serve a therapeutic function by creating an environment based upon trust rather than strict control

C. the inmates at these institutions are often engaged in public works activities
D. the work experiences they provide directly relate to those the prisoner will face in the real world

6. In the United States, the LARGEST group of persons held in jail are those arrested for

   A. drunkenness
   B. disorderly conduct
   C. larceny
   D. drug offenses

7. The systems model of a correctional education program reaches a *visible* stage when

   A. plans are made
   B. cost is estimated
   C. a search is made for sources of funding
   D. a funding request is granted

8. Of the following, the LOWEST stratum in prison subculture is occupied by

   A. bank robbers
   B. forgers
   C. drug addicts
   D. sex offenders

9. All of the following are characteristics of most of the institutions for sentenced adult prisoners in the United States EXCEPT that they are

   A. architecturally antiquated
   B. overcrowded
   C. located within metropolitan areas
   D. too large for effective management

10. A correctional program should have measurable objectives so that its success can be evaluated.
    Of the following, it would be MOST difficult to measure the

    A. change in attitude toward work and study resulting from participation in a correctional program
    B. percentage of participants who obtain employment after release
    C. sum of money earned in a work release program
    D. change in reading level during an educational program

11. The one of the following which should be developed FIRST in establishing a successful training program is the

    A. content of the training program
    B. facilities for giving training
    C. qualification requirements for staff
    D. agency goals and programs

12. Which of the following statements BEST describes the present role of the courts in respect to rehabilitation in correctional institutions? The courts are

    A. ready to abandon their "hands off" policy and take a more active role in institutional affairs
    B. deferring to correctional administrators who have the expertise as well as the responsibility for care, custody and treatment of defendants

C. so busy with backlogs of cases that correctional problems occupy a low priority
D. assuming legal responsibility for institutions located in their jurisdictions

13. All of the following statements concerning the money bail system are correct EXCEPT

    A. under the bail system persons may be confined for crimes for which they are later acquitted
    B. members of organized criminal syndicates have little difficulty in posting bail although they are often dangerous
    C. bail is recognized in the law solely as a method of keeping dangerous persons in jail
    D. the bail system discriminates against poor defendants

14. Daytop Village is a treatment program in the city for

    A. drug offenders
    B. sex offenders
    C. mentally retarded offenders
    D. abused children of offenders

15. In the United States, MOST dollars, manpower, and attention in the correctional field have been invested in

    A. traditional institutional services outside the mainstream of urban life
    B. innovative correctional programming at large state institutions
    C. programs for local jails
    D. community based programs

16. Which of the following is the *single* MOST important source of statistics on crime in the United States today?

    A. FBI Quarterly Review
    B. Uniform Crime Reports of the FBI
    C. Journal of Police Science and Criminal Statistics
    D. Federal Report on Criminal Statistics

17. Reading materials can help correctional staff to better understand the attitudes of inmates toward incarceration. SOUL ON ICE, a penetrating story of one man's reaction to California's prisons, was written by

    A. Malcolm X   B. Huey Newton
    C. Bobby Seale   D. Eldridge Cleaver

Questions 18-20.

DIRECTIONS: Answer Questions 18 through 20 SOLELY on the basis of the following passage:

The basic disparity between punitive and correctional crime control should be noted. The first explicitly or implicitly assumes the availability of choice or freedom of the will and asserts the responsibility of the individual for what he does. Thus the concept of punishment has both a moral and practical justification. However, correctional crime control, though also deterministic in outlook, either explicitly or implicitly considers criminal behavior as the result of conditions and factors present in the individual or his environment; it does not think in terms of free choices available to the individual and his resultant responsibility, but rather in terms of the removal of the criminogenic conditions for which the individual may not be responsible and over which he may not have any control. Some efforts have been made to achieve a theoretical reconciliation of these two rather diametrically opposed approaches but this has not been accomplished, and their coexistence in practice remains an unresolved contradiction.

18. According to the "correctional" view of crime control mentioned in the above passage, criminal behavior is the result of

    A. environmental factors for which individuals should be held responsible
    B. harmful environmental factors which should be eliminated
    C. an individual's choice for which he should be held responsible and punished
    D. an individual's choice and can be corrected in a therapeutic environment

19. According to the above passage, the one of the following which is a *problem* in correctional practice is

    A. identifying emotionally disturbed individuals
    B. determining effective punishment for criminal behavior
    C. reconciling the punitive and correctional views of crime control
    D. assuming that a criminal is the product of his environment and has no free will

20. According to the above passage, the one of the following which is an *assumption* underlying the punitive crime control viewpoint rather than the correctional viewpoint is that crime is caused by

    A. inherited personality traits
    B. poor socio-economic background
    C. lack of parental guidance
    D. irresponsibility on the part of the individual

KEY (CORRECT ANSWERS)

1. A
2. B
3. D
4. D
5. D

6. A
7. D
8. D
9. C
10. A

11. D
12. A
13. C
14. A
15. A

16. B
17. D
18. B
19. C
20. D

TEST 3

Questions 1-6

DIRECTIONS: Answer Questions 1 through 6 SOLELY on the basis of the following selection:

Man's historical approach to criminals can be conveniently summarized as a succession of three R's: Revenge, Restraint, and Reformation. Revenge was the primary response prior to the first revolution in penology in the 18th and 19th centuries. It was replaced during that revolution by an emphasis upon restraint. When the second revolution occurred in the late 19th and 20th centuries, reformation became an important objective. Attention was focused upon the mental and emotional makeup of the offender and efforts were made to alter these as the primary sources of difficulty.

We have now entered yet another revolution in which a fourth concept has been added to the list of R's: Reintegration. This has come about because students of corrections feel that a singular focus upon reforming the offender is inadequate. Successful rehabilitation is a two-sided coin, including reformation on one side and reintegration on the other.

It can be argued that the third revolution is premature. Society itself is still very ambivalent about the offender. It has never really replaced all vestiges of revenge or restraint, simply supplemented them. Thus, while it is unwilling to kill or lock up all offenders permanently, it is also unwilling to give full support to the search for alternatives.

1. According to the above passage, revolutions against accepted treatment of criminals have resulted in all of the following approaches to handling criminals EXCEPT

    A. revenge   B. restraint   C. reformation   D. reintegration

2. According to the above passage, society *now* views the offender with

    A. uncertainty   B. hatred   C. sympathy   D. acceptance

3. According to the above passage, the second revolution directed *particular* attention to

    A. preparing the offender for his return to society
    B. making the pain of punishment exceed the pleasure of crime
    C. exploring the inner feelings of the offender
    D. restraining the offender from continuing his life of crime

4. According to the above passage, students of corrections feel that the *lack* of success of rehabilitation programs is due to

    A. the mental and emotional makeup of the offender
    B. vestiges of revenge and restraint which linger in correction programs
    C. failure to achieve reintegration together with reformation
    D. premature planning of the third revolution

5. The above passage *suggests* that the latest revolution will

    A. fail and the cycle will begin again with revenge or restraint
    B. be the last revolution
    C. not work unless correctional goals can be defined
    D. succumb to political and economic pressures

6. The one of the following titles which BEST expresses the *main* idea of the above passage is:

    A. Is Criminal Justice Enough?
    B. Approaches in the Treatment of the Criminal Offender
    C. The Three R's in Criminal Reformation
    D. Mental Disease Factors in the Criminal Correction System

Questions 7-12.

DIRECTIONS: Answer Questions 7 through 12 SOLELY on the basis of the following selection:

In a study by J. E. Cowden, an attempt was made to determine which variables would best predict institutional adjustment and recidivism in recently committed delinquent boys. The results suggested in particular that older boys, when first institutionalized, who are initially rated as being more mature and more amenable to change, will most likely adjust better than the average boy adjusts to the institution. Prediction of institutional adjustment was rendered slightly more accurate by using the variables of age and personality prognosis in combined form.

With reference to the prediction of recidivism, boys who committed more serious offenses showed less recidivism than average. These boys were also older than average when first committed. The variable of age accounts in part for both their more serious offenses and for their lower subsequent rate of recidivism.

The results also showed some trends suggesting that boys from higher socioeconomic backgrounds tended to commit more serious offenses leading to their institutionalization as delinquents. However, neither the ratings of socioeconomic status nor "home-environment" appeared to be significantly related to recidivism in this study.

Cowden also found an essentially linear relationship between personality prognosis and recidivism, and between institutional adjustment and recidivism. When these variables were used jointly to predict recidivism, accuracy of prediction was increased only slightly, but in general the ability to predict recidivism fell far below the ability to predict institutional adjustment.

7. According to the above passage, which one of the following was NOT found to be a significant factor in predicting recidivism?

    A. Age
    B. Personality
    C. Socioeconomic background
    D. Institutional adjustment

8. According to the above passage, institutional adjustment was *more* accurately predicted when the variables used were

    A. socioeconomic background and recidivism
    B. recidivism and personality
    C. personality and age
    D. age and socioeconomic background

9. According to the above passage, which of the following were *variables* in predicting both recidivism and institutional adjustment?

   A. Age and personality
   B. Family background and age
   C. Nature of offense and age
   D. Personality

10. Which one of the following conclusions is MOST justified by the above passage?

    A. Institutional adjustment had a lower level of predictability than recidivism.
    B. Recidivism and seriousness of offense are negatively correlated to some degree.
    C. Institutional adjustment and personality prognosis, when considered together, are significantly better predictors of recidivism than either one alone.
    D. A delinquent boy from a lower class family background is more likely to have committed a serious first offense than a delinquent boy from a higher socioeconomic background.

11. The study discussed in the passage found that delinquent boys from a higher socioeconomic background tended to

    A. commit more serious crimes
    B. commit less serious crimes
    C. show more recidivism than average
    D. show less recidivism than average

12. The *most appropriate* conclusion to be drawn from the study discussed above is that

    A. delinquent boys from higher socioeconomic backgrounds show less institutional adjustment than average
    B. a high positive correlation was found between recidivism and institutional adjustment
    C. home environment, although not significantly related to recidivism, did influence institutional adjustment
    D. older boys are more likely to commit more serious first offenses and show less recidivism than younger boys

Questions 13-18.

DIRECTIONS: Answer Questions 13 to 18 SOLELY on the basis of the information contained in the following charts and notes.

CHART I
Number of Inmates Enrolled in Libertyville's
Basic Office Skills Program

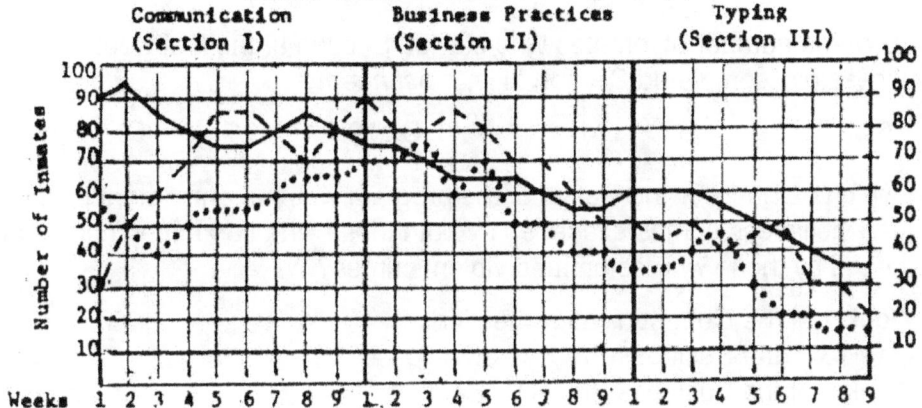

Symbol   Crime Category
―――――   Victimless Crimes
― ― ―   Crimes Against Property
·······   Violent Crimes

NOTES: Inmates can enter a section of the program at any point. Inmates can complete a section of the program at any point by passing an examination.

Enrollment at the end of a section does not necessarily indicate successful completion of that section.

CHART II
Number of Inmates Who Successfully Completed
Each Section of Libertyville's
Office Skills Program

Crime Category	Completed Section I	Completed	Completed Section III
Victimless Crimes	78	55	37
Crimes Against Property	43	57	28
Violent Crimes	80	50	18

CHART III
Percentage of Recidivism Within First Year of Parole
Among Inmates Who Successfully Completed
Various Stages of Libertyville's
Office Skills Program

Crime Category	Completed Section I	Completed Section II	Completed Section III
Victimless Crimes	40%	30%	15%
Crimes Against Property	30%	15%	5%
Violent Crimes	35%	25%	10%

13. The percentage of inmates who successfully completed Section I and were recidivists is, most nearly,

   A. 21%   B. 35%   C. 38%   D. 47%

14. The ratio of the number of inmates who started Section III the first week to the number who successfully completed Section III is, most nearly,

   A. 1.5:1   B. 1.7:1   C. 2.1:1   D. 2.5:1

15. During which of the following weeks of the program was the enrollment by those who committed victimless crimes *exceeded* by both those who committed crimes against property and by those who committed violent crimes?

   A. Week 1 of the Communication Section
   B. Week 3 of the Business Practices Section
   C. Week 9 of the Business Practices Section
   D. Week 6 of the Typing Section

16. If the average number of inmates enrolled in any stage of the program is considered to be the number of inmates enrolled during week 5 of that Section, what is the difference between the average number of inmates enrolled in Section I and in Section III?

   A. 90   B. 125   C. 190   D. 215

17. Assume that 60 percent of the inmates who completed Section III of the Office Skills Program enrolled the first week of the program and completed all three sections of the program. The percent of the initial enrollees who completed the ENTIRE Office Skills Program was, most nearly,

   A. 21%   B. 28%   C. 36%   D. 49%

18. The one of the following periods which exhibits the GREATEST percentage change in enrollment of inmates in the crimes against property category is weeks

   A. 1 to 2 in the Communication Section
   B. 2 to 4 in the Communication Section
   C. 4 to 6 in the Business Practices Section
   D. 3 to 4 in the Typing Section

19. A recent study of the bail system as it is administered conducted by the Legal Aid Society, concluded that the one of the following factors which has the STRONGEST impact on an accused person's chances of being convicted is

   A. whether the person is detained or released prior to trial
   B. the weight of evidence against the person
   C. the type and seriousness of the alleged crime
   D. whether the person has a criminal record

20. Of the following, the *chief* DISADVANTAGE of using on-the-job training is that it 20.____
    A. is initially more costly than using other types of training
    B. is often carried on with little or no planning
    C. requires the worker to remain in the environment in which he will be working
    D. prevents the trainee from obtaining the benefits of a professional's experience

KEY (CORRECT ANSWERS)

1.	A	11.	A
2.	A	12.	D
3.	C	13.	B
4.	C	14.	B
5.	C	15.	B
6.	B	16.	A
7.	C	17.	B
8.	C	18.	A
9.	A	19.	A
10.	B	20.	B

EXAMINATION SECTION
TEST 1

DIRECTIONS: Each question or incomplete statement is followed by several suggested answers or completions. Select the one that BEST answers the question or completes the statement. *PRINT THE LETTER OF THE CORRECT ANSWER IN THE SPACE AT THE RIGHT.*

1. Which one of the following "suggestions to interviewers" should be AVOIDED?　　1.____

    A. Encourage the client to verbalize his thoughts and feelings.
    B. Cover as much as possible in each interview.
    C. Don't hesitate to refer the client to someone else who might be more helpful in the situation.
    D. The problem which is presented initially, or the one which seems most obvious, often is not the real one.

2. If it seems clear that disturbance in parents' marital relationships is a major factor in causing a child to be emotionally disturbed, the counselor should　　2.____

    A. point this out to the parents and tell them that for the welfare of their children, they should resolve their difficulties
    B. suggest that he will be willing to discuss their marital difficulties with them
    C. ignore this and concentrate on helping the child
    D. tactfully suggest that their marital difficulties may be playing a part in their child's disturbance and offer to refer the parents to a qualified marriage counseling service

3. The process of collecting, analyzing, synthesizing and interpreting information about the client should be　　3.____

    A. completed prior to counseling
    B. completed early in the counseling process
    C. limited to counseling which is primarily diagnostic in purpose
    D. continuous throughout counseling

4. Catharsis, the "emotional unloading" of the client's feelings, has a value in the early stages of counseling because it accomplishes all BUT which one of the following goals?　　4.____

    A. It relieves strong physiological tensions in the client.
    B. It increases the client's anxiety and therefore his motivation to continue counseling.
    C. It provides a verbal substitute for "acting out" the client's aggressive feelings.
    D. It releases emotional energy which the client has been using to maintain his defenses.

5. During the first interview, the counselor can expect the client to participate at his BEST when the counselor　　5.____

    A. structures the nature of the counseling process
    B. attempts to summarize the client's problem for him
    C. allows the client to verbalize at his own pace
    D. tells the client that he understands the presenting problem

6. To obtain the most effective results in change of attitude and behavior through parent education, the leader should be

   A. thoroughly grounded in the whole field of psychology
   B. able to help members of the group look at their own attitudes and behavior in constructive ways
   C. completely confident as to the right solution to problems that may be brought up
   D. a warm, charming, friendly human being

7. A social worker's report about a client states that a mother has ambivalent feelings concerning her child. This means that the mother

   A. has contradictory emotional reactions concerning her child
   B. is overprotective of the child
   C. strongly rejects the child
   D. is unduly apprehensive about the child's welfare

8. A psychological report notes, "The client shows little effect." This means that the client

   A. did not take the test too seriously
   B. did not show emotional behavior in situations which normally call for such reactions
   C. did not show signs of fatigue as the testing progressed
   D. reacted to the test situation in a generally favorable manner

9. A psychologist's report states, in part, that a client exhibits some masochistic symptoms. This will be evident to the counselor through the client's persistent attempts at

   A. self-assertion
   B. self-effacement
   C. inflicting physical harm on others
   D. sexual molestation of others of the same sex

10. According to research studies, the type of counselor response that is MOST often followed by a client's expression of insight or illumination is

    A. clarification of feeling
    B. reflection of feeling
    C. simple acceptance
    D. exploratory question

11. Of the following, the BEST way to deal with a 12-year-old boy who feels inferior to his peers is to

    A. provide tasks which he can master with little difficulty
    B. show him how irrational his feelings are
    C. accept his declarations of lack of confidence sympathetically
    D. carefully arrange situations in which he will be obliged to show leadership

12. In counseling or psychotherapy, the factor which is the MOST important for success tends to be the

    A. counselor's theoretical orientation
    B. counselor's attitudes and feelings toward the client

C. techniques used by the counselor
D. amount of experience and training possessed by the counselor

13. Transference is an important aspect of

    A. test construction
    B. grade placement
    C. anecdotal record keeping
    D. therapy

14. The MOST desirable way of establishing rapport with a client who comes to the counselor with a problem is to

    A. demonstrate sincere interest in him
    B. offer to do everything possible to solve his problem for him
    C. use the language of the client
    D. promise to keep his problem confidential

15. Role playing has been used as a technique in parent education work. Of the following, the major value is that it

    A. permits parents to express unconscious feelings and thereby solve conflicts
    B. tells a story in a forceful and therefore lasting way
    C. provides an opportunity for the individual to view his problems by standing off and looking at them through the eyes of someone else
    D. brings to light problems people never knew they had

16. If during a counseling situation a client expressed anger about a particular situation, which of the following responses would a non-directive counselor MOST likely make?

    A. "Why are you so angry?"
    B. "Is there any need to get so upset about this?"
    C. "This has really made you very mad, hasn't it?"
    D. "Do you feel better now that you have expressed your anger?"

17. In a counseling process, the counselor should usually give information

    A. whenever it is needed
    B. at the end of the process
    C. in the introductory interview
    D. just before the client would ordinarily request it

18. "After having recognized and clarified feelings and conflicts, it is usually necessary to go beyond the stage of understanding and to elaborate a constructive plan for future action." Which of the following people would NOT go along with the above statement?

    A. Thorne
    B. Robinson
    C. Williamson
    D. Rogers

19. The counselor should focus his attention in the beginning upon

    A. the transference phenomenon
    B. evidences of hostility
    C. the unique characteristics of the particular relationship at hand
    D. indications of client aggressiveness

20. A recent guidance text that stresses the broad developments of our national heritage, our contemporary social setting, our value patterns, and also the integration into guidance of many disciplines-sociology, anthropology, philosophy, psychology-is

    A. FOUNDATIONS OF GUIDANCE - Miller
    B. GUIDANCE POLICY AND PRACTICE - Mathewson
    C. GUIDANCE IN TODAY'S SCHOOLS - Mortenson & Schmuller
    D. GUIDANCE SERVICES - Humphreys, Traxler & North

20.____

21. Which one of the following characteristics of counseling is inconsistent with the others?

    A. Counseling is more than advice-giving.
    B. Counseling involves something more than the solution to an immediate problem.
    C. Counseling concerns itself with attitudes rather than actions.
    D. Counseling involves intellectual rather than emotional attitudes as its basic raw material.

21.____

22. One approach to counseling has been labeled "non-directive". The word "non-directive" derives from the fact that, in this approach to counseling, the counselor

    A. does not tell the client what he should do
    B. makes the client responsible for the direction of the course of the interviews
    C. does not make judgments about the behavior of the client
    D. avoids possible areas of threat to the client

22.____

23. Of the following personality traits, which would be LEAST essential for an effective counselor to possess?

    A. Extroversion   B. Objectivity
    C. Security   D. Sensitivity

23.____

24. Interpretation as a therapeutic tool is considered a hindrance to therapy progress by

    A. orthodox Freudians   B. neo-analysts
    C. Rogerians   D. Adlerians

24.____

25. The current interpersonal behavior of the client is probably MOST important as a therapy topic to which two analytic theorists?

    A. Freud and Adler   B. Adler and Rank
    C. Freud and Rank   D. Horney and Sullivan

25.____

KEY (CORRECT ANSWERS)

1. B
2. D
3. D
4. B
5. C

6. B
7. A
8. B
9. B
10. C

11. A
12. B
13. D
14. A
15. C

16. C
17. A
18. D
19. C
20. A

21. D
22. B
23. A
24. C
25. D

TEST 2

DIRECTIONS: Each question or incomplete statement is followed by several suggested answers or completions. Select the one that BEST answers the question or completes the statement. *PRINT THE LETTER OF THE CORRECT ANSWER IN THE SPACE AT THE RIGHT.*

1. When a counselor is listening to a client, it is MOST important that he be able to

    A. show interest and agreement with what the client is saying
    B. paraphrase what the client is saying
    C. understand the significance of what the client is saying
    D. differentiate between fact and fiction in what the client is saying

2. On which one of the following is successful counseling LEAST likely to depend?

    A. The counselor's theoretical orientation
    B. The counselor's ability to bring the client's feelings and attitudes into the open
    C. The counselor's diagnostic ability
    D. The client's readiness for counseling

3. A client is referred to you for counseling against his will and is suspicious and uncooperative. You should

    A. explain to him that you cannot help him unless he is prepared to cooperate
    B. explain that you are not taking sides and that you will be impartial
    C. show him that you know how he feels and encourage him to talk about it
    D. explain that you are on his side and will listen sympathetically to anything that he might care to bring up

4. Which one of the following would NOT be considered a basic objective of the first interview between a client and a counselor?

    A. Beginning a sound counseling relationship
    B. Identifying the client's real problem
    C. Opening up the area of client feelings and attitudes
    D. Clarifying the nature of the counseling process for the client

5. All of the following counselor statements or actions are appropriate techniques for ending an interview EXCEPT

    A. "Our time is nearly up. Is there something else you have in mind for today?"
    B. "Let's see now. Suppose we go over what we've accomplished today."
    C. Counselor may glance at his watch and say, "When would you like to come in again?"
    D. Counselor may shuffle papers on desk and say, "Now, let's see; when is my next appointment?"

6. It has been recognized in recent literature that the value structure of the individual counselor has what kind of effect on the counseling process?

    A. Direct
    B. Indirect
    C. Little
    D. None

7. The intensive study of the same individuals over a fairly long period of time represents the

    A. cross-sectional approach
    B. longitudinal approach
    C. clinical approach
    D. biographical approach

8. Of the following techniques, the one which is MOST characteristic of non-directive or client-centered therapy is

    A. encouraging transference
    B. free association
    C. reflection of feeling
    D. permissive questioning

9. In making predictions about how a client will behave in a given situation, a counselor

    A. should limit himself to those situations for which "actuarial" data are available
    B. must rely on "clinical" judgment in many situations but use "actuarial" data wherever possible
    C. should rely on "clinical" judgment in all situations, since they are more valid than "actuarial" predictions
    D. always uses "actuarial" data, but modifies them in light of his "clinical" impression of the client

10. A research study that establishes an hypothesis, sets up control groups, collects data, and generalizes from the data is

    A. formulative
    B. diagnostic
    C. experimental
    D. exploratory

11. The MOST usable single index of the social and economic status of all the members of any family is

    A. occupation of the father
    B. religious affiliation of the family
    C. location of the home in the community
    D. socio-economic rating by neighbors

12. When a counselor does NOT understand the meaning of a response that a counselee has made, the counselor usually should

    A. proceed to another topic
    B. admit his lack of understanding and ask for clarification
    C. act as if he understands so that the counselee's confidence in him is not shaken
    D. ask the counselee to choose his words more carefully

13. When the counselor makes a response which touches off a high degree of resistance in the counselee, he should

    A. apologize and rephrase his remark in a less threatening manner
    B. accept the resistance
    C. ignore the counselee's resistance
    D. recognize that little more will be accomplished in the interview and offer another appointment

14. Directive and non-directive counseling are two emphases in counseling theory and practice. From the pairs of names listed below, indicate the two that are representative of the Directive school.

    A. Thorne and Williamson
    B. Rogers and Thorne
    C. Williamson and Sullivan
    D. Sullivan and Rogers

15. Rogerian counseling theory is based on the assumption that the potential and tendency for growth toward a fully functioning personality is present in

    A. a few "self-actualized" persons
    B. most people of above average intelligence
    C. people whose behavior can be considered as "normal" and socially effective
    D. all people

16. Anecdotal records should contain which type(s) of information?

    A. Evaluations
    B. Interpretations
    C. Factual reports
    D. Prognoses

17. RESISTANCE in relation to psychological counseling typically refers to the

    A. client's defenses against his inner conflicts
    B. counselor's unwillingness to deal with the client's emotional problems
    C. client's having enough ego strength so that he can face his problems
    D. counselor's having enough ego strength so that he can help the client face his problems

18. On which one of the following does the democratic leader specifically rely? His ability to

    A. listen and tactfully guide the discussion in the direction he has planned and the members' willingness to cooperate
    B. diagnose situations, to interpret and explain them to the members and their willingness to accept
    C. discern the issues which the members could profitably discuss and his willingness to allow them with his help to do so
    D. understand the meaning of the response from the member's frame of reference and his willingness for them to make decisions

19. Advisement in counseling is MOST effective when the counselee is in a state of

    A. perceiving his problem as related to a conflict with inner forces
    B. minimal conflict and of optimal readiness for action
    C. perceiving his problem as related to an external conflict
    D. feeling extremely ambivalent about his self-concept

20. Of the following, the MOST valid use of projective techniques is the study of the

    A. problems which an individual faces
    B. cultural effects upon an individual
    C. inner world of an individual
    D. human relationships of an individual

21. Diagnosis is NOT regarded as a helpful antecedent to counseling by

   A. Cottle
   B. Rogers
   C. Thorne
   D. Williamson

22. The beginning counselor must be alert to interferences to rapport. Which one of the following is NOT considered an intereference?

   A. Injecting the counselor's present mood
   B. Engaging in "small talk" at the start of the interview
   C. Registering surprise or dismay
   D. Emphasizing the counselor's ability

23. There is some evidence according to Rogers that counseling is more effective with

   A. younger adults or higher intelligence
   B. older adults of higher intelligence
   C. younger adults of lower intelligence
   D. older adults of lower intelligence

24. In assisting with the scheduling of interviews for educational planning, the counselor should suggest that group instruction

   A. follow the counseling interview
   B. is not necessary when individual interviews can be scheduled since each case is different
   C. precede the counseling
   D. may either precede or follow the counseling interview

25. A client has requested an interview with the counselor to discuss a personal problem. In general, the BEST way to begin the interview is to

   A. come directly to the point and encourage the client to talk about his problem
   B. assure him that everything discussed will be confidential
   C. offer to help him in every way possible
   D. inquire whether he has discussed the problem with anyone else

KEY (CORRECT ANSWERS)

1.	C		11.	A
2.	A		12.	B
3.	C		13.	B
4.	B		14.	A
5.	D		15.	D
6.	A		16.	C
7.	B		17.	A
8.	C		18.	C
9.	B		19.	B
10.	C		20.	C

21.	B
22.	B
23.	A
24.	C
25.	A

EXAMINATION SECTION
TEST 1

DIRECTIONS: Each question or incomplete statement is followed by several suggested answers or completions. Select the one that BEST answers the question or completes the statement. *PRINT THE LETTER OF THE CORRECT ANSWER IN THE SPACE AT THE RIGHT.*

1. The one of the following which is the BEST description of a properly objective investigator is one who

    A. is friendly and sensitive to the client's feelings, without becoming emotionally involved
    B. is distant and impersonal, remaining unaffected by what the client says
    C. lets personal emotions enter as far as the client's situation calls for them
    D. becomes emotionally involved with the client's situation but without showing this involvement

2. The one of the following which is MOST necessary for successfully interviewing a person who belongs to a culture different from that of the investigator is for the investigator to

    A. have some appreciation of the other culture
    B. ignore those cultural differences which lead to bias
    C. stay away from sensitive, "touchy" issues
    D. assume the mannerisms of people in the other cultures

3. In fact-finding interviews, it is generally assumed that the smaller the number of interviewees, the greater the increase of reliability with the addition of others. The PROPER number of interviewees needed to insure the accuracy of information obtained *generally* depends upon the

    A. educational level of those interviewed
    B. number of people who have the required information
    C. directness of the questions asked
    D. variability of the information received

4. The one of the following which is generally MOST likely to be accurately described in an interview by an interviewee is

    A. the presence of a large painting in the investigator's office
    B. the number of people in the investigator's waiting room
    C. space relations
    D. duration of time

5. The one of the following which is *generally* the BEST course of action for an investigator to take when interviewing a person who is reluctant to tell what he knows about a matter under investigation is to

    A. be curt and abrupt and threaten the person with the consequences of his withholding information
    B. be firm and severe and pressure the person into telling the needed information
    C. be patient and candid with the person being questioned about the investigation since doing otherwise is not ethical

D. give the person false information about the investigation so he will give the needed information without realizing its importance

6. It is often recommended that an investigator prepare in advance a list of questions or topics to be covered in an interview. The MAIN reason for using such a check list is to

A. allow investigations to be assigned to less efficient investigators
B. eliminate a large amount of follow-up paper work
C. aid the investigator in remembering to cover all important topics
D. aid the investigator in maintaining an objective distance from the person interviewed

7. Usually, the CHIEF advantage of a directive approach in an interview is that

A. the investigator maintains control over the course of the interview
B. the person interviewed is more likely to be put at ease
C. the person interviewed is generally left free to direct the interview
D. the investigator will not suggest answers to the person interviewed

8. Usually, the CHIEF advantage of a non-directive approach by an investigator in conducting an interview is that

A. the investigator generally conceals what he is looking for in the interview
B. the person interviewed is more likely to express his true feelings about the topic under discussion
C. the person interviewed is more likely to follow an idea introduced by the investigator
D. the investigator can keep the discussion limited to topics he believes to be relevant

9. The one of the following which is generally the *least likely* to be accurate in a description of an event given to an investigator is a statement about

A. the presence of an object
B. the number of people, when their number is small
C. locations of people
D. duration of time

10. Assume that you, an investigator, are conducting a character investigation. In an interview, the one of the following character traits of the person being interviewed which can USUALLY be determined with a *good* degree of reliability is

A. honesty
B. dependability
C. forcefulness
D. perseverance

11. As an investigator, you have been assigned the task of obtaining a family's social history. The BEST place for you to interview members of the family while obtaining this social history would *generally* be in

A. the family's home
B. your agency's general offices
C. the home of a friend of the family
D. your own private office

12. You, an investigator, are checking someone's work history. The way for you to get the MOST reliable information from a previous employer is to

    A. send personal letters; the employer will respond to the personal attention
    B. send form letters; the employer will cooperate readily since little time or effort is asked of him
    C. arrange a personal interview; the employer may offer information he would not care to put in a letter or speak over the phone
    D. telephone; this method is as effective as a personal interview and is much more convenient

13. The effect that attestation, or the formal taking of an oath, has on witness testimony is to

    A. decrease accuracy, since a witness under oath is more nervous about what is said
    B. make little difference, since the witness is not too swayed by an oath
    C. increase accuracy, since a witness under oath feels more responsibility for what is said
    D. eliminate inaccuracy unless there is deliberate perjury on the part of the witness

14. If an investigator obtains testimony from persons in interviews by means of interrogation or asking questions rather than by letting the person freely relate the testimony, what is said will GENERALLY be

    A. greater in range and less accurate
    B. greater in range and more accurate
    C. about the same in range and less accurate
    D. about the same in range and more accurate

15. Experienced investigators have learned to phrase their questions carefully in order to obtain the desired response. Of the following, the question which would *usually* elicit the MOST accurate answer is:

    A. "How old are you?"
    B. "What is your income?"
    C. "How are you today?"
    D. "What is the date of your birth?"

16. The one of the following questions which would *generally* lead to the LEAST reliable answer is

    A. "Did you see a wallet?"
    B. "Was the German Shepherd gray?"
    C. "Didn't you see the stop sign?"
    D. "Did you see the guard on duty?"

17. Some investigators may make a practice of observing details of the surroundings when interviewing in someone's home or office. Such a practice is *generally* considered

    A. *undesirable,* mainly because such snooping is an unwarranted, unethical invasion of privacy
    B. *undesirable,* mainly because useful information is rarely, if ever, gained this way
    C. *desirable,* mainly because, useful insights into the character of the person interviewed may be gained

D. *desirable,* mainly because it is impossible to evaluate a person adequately without such observation of his environment

18. The one of the following questions which will MOST often lead to a reliable answer is:

    A. "Was his hair very dark?"
    B. "Wasn't there a clock on the wall?"
    C. "Was the automobile white or gray?"
    D. "Did you see a motorcycle?"

19. The one of the following which can MOST accurately be determined by an investigator by means of interviewing is

    A. a persons's intelligence
    B. factual information about an event
    C. a person's aptitude for a specific task
    D. a person's perceptions of his own abilities

20. The one of the following which is *most likely* to help a person being interviewed feel at ease is for the investigator to

    A. let him start the conversation
    B. give him an abundance of time
    C. be relaxed himself
    D. open the interview by telling a joke

21. If the interviewee is to perceive some goal for himself in the interview and thus be motivated to participate in it, it is important that he clearly understand some of the aspects of the interview. Of the following aspects, the one the interviewee needs LEAST to understand is

    A. the purpose of the interview
    B. the mechanics of interviewing
    C. the use made of the information he contributes
    D. what will be expected of him in the interview

22. As an investigator working on a project requiring inter-agency cooperation, you find that employees of an agency involved in the project are constantly making it difficult for you to obtain necessary information. Of the following, the BEST action for you to take FIRST is to

    A. discuss the problem with your supervisor
    B. speak with your counterpart in the other agency
    C. discuss the problem with the head of the uncooperative agency
    D. contact the head of your agency

23. The investigator is justified in misleading the interviewee only when, in the investigator's judgment, this is clearly required by the problem being investigated. Such practice is

    A. *necessary;* there are times when complete honesty will impede a successful investigation
    B. *unnecessary ;* such a tactic is unethical and should never be employed
    C. *necessary;* an investigator must be guided by success rather than ethical considerations in an investigation

D. *unnecessary;* it is clearly doubtful whether such a practice will help the investigator conclude the investigation successfully

24. Assume that, in investigating a case of possible welfare fraud, it becomes necessary to hold an interview in the client's home in order to observe family interaction and conditions. Upon arriving, the investigator finds that the client's living room is noisy and crowded, with neighbors present and children running in and out. Of the following, the BEST course of action for the investigator to take is to 24.____

   A. conduct the interview in the living room after telling the children to behave, and asking the neighbors to leave
   B. tell the client that it is impossible to conduct the interview in the apartment, and make an appointment for the next day in the investigator's office
   C. suggest that they move from the living room into the kitchen where there is a table on which he can write
   D. try his best to conduct the interview in the noisy and crowded living room

25. You, an investigator, are giving testimony in court about a matter you have investigated. An attorney is questioning you in an abrasive, badgering way, and, in an insulting manner, calls into doubt your ability as an investigator. You lose your temper and respond angrily, telling the attorney to stop harassing and insulting you. Of the following, the BEST description of such a response is that it is *generally* 25.____

   A. *appropriate;* as a witness in court, you do not have to take insults from anybody, including an attorney
   B. *inappropriate; losing your* temper will show that you are weak and cannot be trusted as an investigator
   C. *appropriate;* a judge and jury will usually respect someone who responds strongly to unjust provocation
   D. *inappropriate;* such conduct is unprofessional and may unfavorably impress a judge and jury

KEY (CORRECT ANSWERS)

1. A
2. A
3. D
4. A
5. C

6. C
7. A
8. B
9. D
10. C

11. A
12. C
13. C
14. A
15. D

16. B
17. C
18. D
19. D
20. C

21. B
22. A
23. A
24. C
25. D

TEST 2

DIRECTIONS: Each question or incomplete statement is followed by several suggested answers or completions. Select the one that BEST answers the question or completes the statement. *PRINT THE LETTER OF THE CORRECT ANSWER IN THE SPACE AT THE RIGHT.*

1. The reliability of information obtained increases with the number of persons interviewed. The more the interviewees differ in their statements, the more persons it is necessary to interview to ascertain the true facts. According to this statement, the dependability of the information about an occurrence obtained from interviews is related to   1._____

   A. how many people are interviewed
   B. how soon after the occurrence an interview can be arranged
   C. the individual technique of the interviewer
   D. the interviewer's ability to detect differences in the statements of interviewees

2. An investigator interviews members of the public at his desk. The attitude of the public toward this department will probably be LEAST affected by this investigator's   2._____

   A. courtesy   B. efficiency
   C. height   D. neatness

3. The *one* of the following which is NOT effective in obtaining complete testimony from a witness during an interview is to   3._____

   A. ask questions in chronological order
   B. permit the witness to structure the interview
   C. make sure you fully understand the response to each question
   D. review questions to be asked beforehand

4. The person MOST likely to be a good interviewer is one who   4._____

   A. is able to outguess the person being interviewed
   B. tries to change the attitudes of the persons he interviews
   C. controls the interview by skillfully dominating the conversation
   D. is able to imagine himself in the position of the person being interviewed

5. When you are interviewing someone to obtain information, the BEST of the following reasons for you to repeat certain of his exact words is to   5._____

   A. *assure* him that appropriate action will be taken
   B. *encourage* him to elaborate on a point he has made
   C. *assure* him that you agree with his point of view
   D. *encourage* him to switch to another topic of discussion

6. You are interviewing a client who has just been assaulted. He has trouble collecting his thoughts and telling his story coherently. Which of the following represents the MOST effective method of questioning under these circumstances?   6._____

   A. Ask questions which structure the client's story chronologically into units, each with a beginning, middle and end.
   B. Ask several questions at a time to structure the interview.

73

C. Ask open-ended questions which allow the client to respond in a variety of ways.
D. Begin the interview with several detailed questions in order to focus the client's attention on the situation.

7. You are conducting an initial interview with a witness who expresses reluctance, even hostility, to being questioned. You feel it would be helpful to take some notes during the interview.
In this situation, it would be BEST to

   A. put off note-taking until a follow-up interview, and concentrate on establishing rapport with the witness
   B. explain the necessity of note-taking, and proceed to take notes during the interview
   C. make notes from memory after the witness has left
   D. take notes, but as unobtrusively as possible

8. You are interviewing the owner of a stolen car about facts relating to the robbery. After completing his statement, the car owner suddenly states that some of the details he has just related are not correct. You realize that this change might be significant.
Of the following, it would be BEST for you to

   A. ask the owner what other details he may have given incorrectly
   B. make a note of the discrepancy for discussion at a later date
   C. repeat your questioning on the details that were misstated until you have covered that area completely
   D. explain to the owner that because of his change of testimony, you will have to repeat the entire interview

9. Assume that you have been asked to get all the pertinent information from an employee who claims that she witnessed a robbery.
Which of the following questions is *least likely* to influence the witness's response?

   A. "Can you describe the robber's hair?"
   B. "Did the robber have a lot of hair?"
   C. "Was the robber's hair black or brown?"
   D. "Was the robber's hair very dark?"

10. In order to obtain an accurate statement from a person who has witnessed a crime, it is BEST to question the witness

    A. as soon as possible after the crime was committed
    B. after the witness has discussed the crime with other witnesses
    C. after the witness has had sufficient time to reflect on events and formulate a logical statement
    D. after the witness has been advised that he is obligated to tell the whole truth

11. Assume that your superior assigns you to interview an individual who, he warns, seems to be hightly "introverted." You should be aware that, during an interview, such a person is likely to

    A. hold views which are highly controversial in nature
    B. be domineering and try to control the direction of the interview
    C. resist answering personal questions regarding his background
    D. give information which is largely fabricated

12. A young woman was stabbed in the hand in her home by her estranged boyfriend. Her mother and two sisters were at home at the time.
    Of the following, it would generally be BEST to interview the young woman in the presence of

    A. her mother *only*
    B. all members of her immediate family
    C. members of the family who actually observed the crime
    D. the official authorities

13. The one of the following statements concerning interviewing which is LEAST valid is that

    A. skill in interviewing can be improved by knowledge of the basic factors involving relations between people
    B. interviewing should become a routine and mechanical practice to the skilled and experienced interviewer
    C. genuine interest in people is essential for successful interviewing
    D. certain psychological traits characterize most people most of the time

14. The initial interview will normally be more of a problem to the interviewer than any subsequent interviews he may have with the same person because

    A. the interviewee is likely to be hostile
    B. there is too much to be accomplished in one session
    C. he has less information about the client than he will have later
    D. some information may be forgotten when later making record of this first interview

15. Continuous taking of notes during an interview is generally

    A. *desirable* because no important facts will be forgotten
    B. *undesirable* because it gives the person being interviewed a clue to the importance of the information being obtained from him
    C. *desirable* because the interviewer cannot write as fast as the person being interviewed can speak
    D. *undesirable* because it may put the person being interviewed ill at ease

16. "Carefully planned interviews tend to impose restrictions which leave little room for spontaneity." A flaw in this critiscism of the planned interview is that it does NOT take into account that

    A. a planned interview obviates the need for spontaneity
    B. even the planned interview may be flexible
    C. not all planned interviews impose restrictions
    D. restrictions that result from planning are undesirable

17. Writing up the interview into a systematic report is BEST done

    A. in the presence of the subject, so that mistakes can be corrected immediately
    B. within a reasonably short time after the interview, so that nothing is forgotten
    C. no sooner than several days after the interview, so that the interviewer will have had plenty of time to think about it
    D. with the help of someone not present at the interview, so that an objective view can be obtained

18. While you are conducting an interview, the telephone on your desk rings. Of the following, it would be BEST for you to

    A. ask the interviewer at the next desk to answer your telephone and take the message for you
    B. excuse yourself, pick up the telephone, and tell the person on the other end you are busy and will call him back later
    C. ignore the ringing telephone and continue with the interview
    D. use another telephone to inform the operator not to put calls through to you while you are conducting an interview

19. An interviewee is at your desk, which is quite near to desks where other people work. He beckons you a little closer and starts to talk in a low voice as though he does not want anyone else to hear him. Under these circumstances, the BEST thing for you to do is to

    A. ask him to speak a little louder so that he can be heard
    B. cut the interview short and not get involved in his problems
    C. explain that people at other desks are not eavesdroppers
    D. listen carefully to what he says and give it consideration

20. Of the following, the BEST way for a person to develop competence as an interviewer is to

    A. attend lectures on interviewing techniques
    B. practice with employees on the job
    C. conduct interviews under the supervision of an experienced instructor
    D. attend a training course in counseling

21. During the course of an interview, it would be LEAST desirable for the investigator to

    A. correct immediately any grammatical errors made by an interviewee
    B. express himself in such a way as to be clearly understood
    C. restrict the interviewee to the subject of the interview
    D. make notes in a way that will not disturb the interviewee

22. Suppose that you are interviewing an eleven year old boy. The CHIEF point among the following for you to keep in mind is that a child, as compared with an adult, is generally

    A. more likely to attempt to conceal information
    B. a person of lower intelligence
    C. more garrulous
    D. more receptive to suggestive questions

23. In interviewing a person, "suggestive questions" should be avoided because, among the following,

    A. the answers to leading questions are not admissible in evidence
    B. an investigator must be fair and impartial
    C. the interrogation of a witness must be formulated according to his mentality
    D. they are less apt to lead to the truth

24. Among the following, it is generally desirable to interview a person outside his home or office because

A. the presence of relatives and friends may prevent him from speaking freely
B. a person's surroundings tend to color his testimony
C. the person will find less distraction outside his home or office
D. a person tends to dominate the interview when in familiar surroundings

25. For the interviewing process to be MOST successful, the interviewer should generally   25._____

   A. remind the person being interviewed that false statements will constitute perjury and will be prosecuted as such
   B. devise a single and unvarying pattern for all interviewing situations
   C. let the individual being interviewed control the content of the interview but not its length
   D. vary his interviewing approach as the situation requires it

---

KEY (CORRECT ANSWERS)

1. A	11. C
2. C	12. D
3. B	13. B
4. D	14. C
5. B	15. D
6. A	16. B
7. B	17. B
8. C	18. B
9. A	19. D
10. A	20. C

21. A
22. D
23. D
24. A
25. D

EXAMINATION SECTION
TEST 1

DIRECTIONS: Each question or incomplete statement is followed by several suggested answers or completions. Select the one that BEST answers the question or completes the statement. *PRINT THE LETTER OF THE CORRECT ANSWER IN THE SPACE AT THE RIGHT.*

Questions 1-20.

DIRECTIONS: Questions 1 through 20 are based on the accompanying reading comprehension section which quotes a portion of the Correction Law, starting on Page 6.

1. Provisions of *Section 212* apply to   1.____

   A. parole and conditional release for all prisoners
   B. conditional release for persons sentenced to reformatories only
   C. parole or conditional release of persons serving indeterminate or reformatory sentences
   D. probation or conditional release for persons incarcerated with fixed minimum sentences

2. Which one of the following does NOT apply to both reformatory and indefinite sentences?   2.____

   A. The parole board's determinations may affect the minimum term of confinement.
   B. The prisoner is entitled to a personal interview and a notice in writing concerning determinations made in respect to his period of confinement.
   C. The board must determine within six months after confinement the minimum date for parole consideration.
   D. If the board does not grant parole at the expiration of the minimum period of confinement, review of parole determinations must be made periodically.

3. The parole board determines minimum prison sentences   3.____

   A. whenever there is an indeterminate sentence
   B. when an indeterminate sentence was imposed and the court did not fix the minimum term
   C. when, in the interests of society, a minimum term should be established
   D. when no minimum term is established for the offense in the penal code

4. In setting a minimum term, the inmate must be afforded   4.____

   A. counsel if he requests it
   B. a quasi-judicial hearing before the entire board
   C. an interview
   D. an opportunity to review the files being considered in arriving at the determination

5. All determinations by individual members of the parole board relating to minimum sentences   5.____

79

A. must be concurred in by all the members of the board
B. are subject to court review as provided to ascertain whether they are arbitrary, unreasonable, or capricious
C. must bear the recommendation of the head of the board of the institution before the determination is deemed to be final
D. are deemed tentative if the minimum term is more than one-third of the maximum sentence or more than three years from the date sentence commenced, whichever is less

6. Which one of the following is NOT a function of the parole board? To

   A. pass upon applications for conditional releases
   B. determine when persons serving indeterminate or reformatory sentences shall be eligible for parole
   C. determine when persons serving an indeterminate sentence with court-fixed minimum terms are eligible for parole
   D. review the minimum sentences prescribed by the courts periodically to determine whether there should be a reduction in such minimum term, provided that the minimum period shall in no case be less than one year

7. The principal purpose of *Section 212 (3)* and *(4)* is

   A. to establish a time schedule for parole considerations
   B. to establish procedures for reconsideration of parole determinations
   C. to establish time schedules for minimum periods of imprisonment
   D. all of the above

8. For persons who have received a reformatory sentence,

   A. the parole board must determine the earliest date prisoner is to be considered for parole
   B. the date established for determination of eligibility for parole is always subject to review
   C. all procedures for reformatory sentences subject to parole are identical with those for prisoners serving indeterminate sentences
   D. the principal difference between parole proceedings for reformatory prisoners and those incarcerated in prisons is that there must be court notification of the actions taken in respect to reformatory inmates

9. Conditional release as defined

   A. is the same as parole in respect to the rules governing eligibility
   B. differs from parole in that parolees' time under parole may be considered for credit against the term of the sentence if there is a revocation
   C. is the same as parole in respect to earned good behavior time
   D. differs from parole in that persons so released continue in legal custody until the expiration of their maximum term

10. Which one of the following is NOT accurate in respect to conditional releases?

    A. The parole board sets the conditions of the release.
    B. With one major exception, the conditions for conditional release and parole are required to be substantially the same.

C. A released inmate is still under the custody of the State Department of Correction.
D. After a specified minimum period, inmates must automatically be considered for conditional release.

11. The procedure governing revocation of parole or conditional release as provided for in this statute requires

    A. a quasi-judicial hearing
    B. a finding of reasonable cause to revoke
    C. that the entire board hear the charges
    D. that the violator be given an opportunity to present witnesses in his defense

12. At a hearing to revoke conditional release or parole, the person charged with violations

    A. may not have counsel
    B. must appear personally
    C. may require that the hearing be held in a place close to his official residence
    D. may not cross-examine the complaining witness

13. In respect to an absolute discharge, which one of the following statements is NOT true?

    A. Such a discharge may be granted at the absolute discretion of the parole board.
    B. It terminates the sentence.
    C. It may be granted when the board feels it to be in the interest of society.
    D. It may be granted to persons serving reformatory sentences as provided for in the penal law.

14. Which one of the following statements is NOT true in respect to sentences imposed prior to September, 2007?

    A. Except for persons convicted of murder one or two, kidnapping, felony drug violations for the third time or any other fourth felony offender, all prisoners are eligible for parole after a minimum period of imprisonment of eight years and four months or sooner.
    B. Eligibility for parole under minimum periods established is computed from date of incarceration after sentencing.
    C. Computations for concurrent and consecutive sentences differ.
    D. No credit is allowed for good conduct except as provided by the laws of 1970 or other provisions of law.

15. For prisoners sentenced prior to September, 2007, in respect to concurrent sentences, in computing minimum time served to ascertain eligibility for parole, the

    A. minimum time required is the sum of the minimum time for each sentence
    B. minimum sentence requirements are met by service of the period that has the longest unexpired time to run
    C. time served on any sentence is to be credited against the minimum period of all the sentences
    D. minimum sentence may be ascertained by a computation of the total time encompassed in the concurrent sentences and by determining the minimum period for a term of that duration

4 (#1)

16. In respect to parole eligibility consideration for persons sentenced prior to September, 2007,

   A. there was an absolute right to be considered for parole
   B. there was an absolute right to parole
   C. eligibility for parole is ascertainable only by reference to the court's sentencing
   D. eligibility for parole is ascertainable only by reference to the penal code

17. Which one of the following statements reflects the thrust of *Section 212-a?*

   A. There is an absolute minimum time that must be served by all prisoners sentenced under the prior penal statute.
   B. Depending upon the category of crime committed, there is a minimum period that a prisoner serves before he must be considered for parole.
   C. Prisoners are entitled to parole within six months after they are eligible.
   D. The section establishes guidelines for determining eligibility for parole, but the ultimate determinations concerning when a prisoner shall be considered eligible for parole remain with the parole board.

18. Which one of the following statements BEST reflects the guidelines established by this statute as the factors to be considered in granting parole or conditional release?

   A. Good conduct in jail is indicative of conduct to be expected from a parolee and is, therefore, an important factor to be considered in determinations governing parole or conditional release.
   B. There are no standards that can be established because each case is different; therefore, the determination to parole must be based upon the discretion of the board.
   C. The standards that guide the board in determining whether to parole or conditionally release a prisoner are that he is not likely to be guilty of criminal behavior while at large and that he will not otherwise so conduct himself that he might endanger others.
   D. Since the primary consideration in parole determinations is whether the parolee can return to society without breaking the law again, the prisoner's good conduct while in jail or efficient performance of duties assigned to him are irrelevant in making parole or conditional release determinations.

19. In making its determinations concerning the release of prisoners, the board

   A. must be satisfied that the prisoner will be suitably employed upon his release at a wage that will sustain him
   B. relies wholly upon reports of the prison officials and physical and psychiatric reports
   C. is bound by the decision of the majority of the members sitting on the case
   D. is bound by the *substantial evidence rule* in arriving at its determination after it examines the record as a whole

20. In establishing conditions for parole, the board

   A. must provide that the parolee remain within the state unless he is given prior approval for travel by the parole officer
   B. may not provide that parole is conditioned upon the parolee's making restitution of monies or goods stolen

C. may be so general that the parolee is subject to the dictates of standards of conduct established not by the board but solely by the parole officer
D. may incorporate both specific rules in regard to the particular parolee as well as rules of general applicability respecting parolees

CORRECTION LAW

§ 212. Parole and conditional release under indeterminate and reformatory sentences.

1. The provisions of this section shall govern, to the exclusion of, other provisions of this article, the duties and powers of the board of parole and the procedures with respect to parole and conditional release and the revocation thereof where an indeterminate or reformatory sentence has been imposed pursuant to the provisions of the penal law as enacted by chapter ten hundred thirty of the laws of nineteen hundred sixty-five, as amended. Matters not expressly covered herein or covered in such penal law shall be governed by such other provisions of law as may be applicable.

2. In any case where a person is received in an institution under the jurisdiction of the state department of correction with an indeterminate sentence, and the court has not fixed the minimum period of imprisonment, the board shall cause to be brought before one or more members not sooner than nine months or later than one year from the date the term of such sentence commenced all information with regard to such person referred to in section two hundred eleven and such of the information specified in subdivision four of section two hundred fourteen of this chapter as may have been compiled. The member or members receiving such information shall study same and shall personally interview the sentenced person. Upon conclusion of the interview, such member or members shall make a determination as to the minimum period of imprisonment to be served prior to parole consideration. Such determination shall have the same force and effect as a minimum period fixed by a court, except that the board may at any time make subsequent determinations reducing such minimum period provided that the period shall in no case be reduced to less than one year. Notification of the determination and of any subsequent determination shall be furnished in writing to the sentenced person and to the person in charge of the institution as soon as practicable.

In any case where the minimum period of imprisonment is fixed, pursuant to this subdivision, at more than one-third of the maximum term, or at more than three years from the date the sentence commenced, whichever is less, such determination shall be deemed tentative and shall be reviewed by the entire board as soon as practicable. Upon any such review, it shall not be necessary for the board members to personally interview the sentenced person, and the decision of a majority of the board shall constitute the determination.

3. At least one month prior to the expiration of the minimum period or periods of imprisonment fixed by the court, or fixed as provided in subdivision two of this section, the board shall determine whether a person serving an indeterminate sentence of imprisonment should be paroled at the expiration of the minimum period or periods. Such determination shall be made in accordance with sections two hundred thirteen and two hundred fourteen of this chapter insofar as consistent with this section. If the board does not grant parole at such time, it shall specify a date not more than twenty-four months from the date of such determination for reconsideration, and the procedures to be followed upon reconsideration shall be the same.

4. In any case where a person is received in an institution under the jurisdiction of the state department of correction with a reformatory sentence, the board shall fix a minimum date for parole consideration within six months from the date the period of such sentence commenced and shall make a determination as to whether parole shall be granted not later than the expiration of such date. The procedures specified in subdivisions two and three of this section shall apply insofar as consistent, except that the initial decision shall be reviewed

by the board if the minimum date is fixed at more than eighteen months from the date the term commenced, and reconsiderations of parole determinations shall be at eighteen month intervals.

5. All requests for conditional release under paragraph (b) of subdivision one of section 70.40 of the penal law shall be made in writing to the board of parole on forms prescribed by the board and furnished by the division of parole. Within one month from the date any such application is received by the board, if it appears that the applicant is eligible for conditional release, or will be eligible for conditional release during such month, the conditions of release shall be fixed in accordance with rules and regulations prescribed by the board. Such conditions shall be substantially the same as the conditions imposed upon parolees, except that time spent under conditional release shall not be credited against the term of the sentence. No person shall be conditionally released unless he has agreed, in writing, to the conditions of release, and any such agreement shall contain the following clause printed immediately above the signature line: I understand and agree that if I am returned to an institution under the jurisdiction of the state department of correction for violation of any of the above conditions, the time spent under conditional release will not be credited against the term of my sentence and that the good behavior time earned by me prior to the date of my conditional release cannot be used as a basis for requesting any subsequent release. I further understand that if I am so returned, I may, however, subsequently receive time allowances against the remaining portion of my maximum or aggregate maximum term not to exceed in the aggregate one-third of such portion provided such remaining portion of my maximum or aggregate maximum term is more than one year and that I shall not again earn any good behavior time against the remaining portion of my sentence if such remaining portion of my sentence is one year or less.

6. Persons paroled and conditionally released from institutions under the jurisdiction of the state department of correction shall, while on parole or conditional release, be in the legal custody of the board of parole until expiration of the maximum term or period of the sentence, or expiration of the period of supervision, or return to such an institution, as the case may be.

7. Whenever there is reasonable cause to believe that a person who is on parole or conditional release has violated the conditions thereof, the board of parole, as soon as practicable, shall declare such person to be delinquent. Thereafter, the board shall at the first available opportunity permit the alleged violator to appear personally, but not through counsel or others, before a panel of three members and explain the alleged violation. Such appearance shall be either at an institution under the jurisdiction of the state department of correction or at such other place as may be designated pursuant to rules and regulations of the board. The board shall within a reasonable time make a determination on any such declaration of delinquency either by dismissing the declaration or revoking the parole or conditional release. If the board dismisses the declaration, the interruptions specified in subdivision three of section 70.40 of the penal law shall not apply, but the time spent in custody in any state or local correctional institution by a person who is on conditional release shall be credited against the term of his sentence in accordance with the rules specified in paragraph (c) of that subdivision.

Revocation of parole or of conditional release shall not prevent re-parole, or re-release provided such re-parole, or re-release is not inconsistent with any other provisions of law.

8. If the board of parole is satisfied that an absolute discharge from parole or from conditional release is in the best interest of society, the board may grant such a discharge prior to

expiration of the full maximum term to any indeterminate sentence parolee who has been on unrevoked parole for at least five consecutive years or to any person who has been on unrevoked conditional release for at least two consecutive years. Discharge of persons under a reformatory sentence may be granted at any time, as provided in the penal law.

A discharge granted under this section shall constitute a termination of the sentence with respect to which it was granted.

9. The provisions of sections sixty-six, two hundred fifteen, two hundred sixteen, two hundred seventeen, two hundred twenty-one, two hundred twenty-two, two hundred twenty-four, two hundred twenty-four-a, two hundred twenty-five, and two hundred eighty-three of this chapter shall apply to parole and conditional release insofar as consistent with this section.

10. The board of parole shall promulgate rules and regulations for the procedures to be followed in carrying out its duties and the duties of the division of parole under this section. Any action taken by the board pursuant to this article shall be deemed a judicial function and shall not be reviewable if done in accordance with law.

11. In any case where a person is entitled to jail time credit under the provisions of paragraph (c) of subdivision three of section 70.40 of the penal law, it shall be the duty of the board of parole, or of such officer as may be designated by the board, to certify to the commissioner of correction the amount of such credit.

§ 212-a. Parole eligibility of certain inmates sentenced for crimes committed prior to September first, two thousand seven.

1. The provisions of this subdivision shall apply in any case where a person is under one or more of the following sentences imposed pursuant to the penal law in effect prior to September first, two thousand seven:

(a) Life imprisonment for the crime of murder in the first degree pursuant to section ten hundred forty-five or section ten hundred forty-five-a of such law;
(b) Life imprisonment for the crime of kidnapping pursuant to section twelve hundred fifty of such law; or
(c) Death commuted to life imprisonment for the crime of murder in the first degree or for the crime of kidnapping pursuant to one of the above sections.

Any such person who is not otherwise or who will not sooner become eligible for release on parole under such sentence shall be or become eligible for release on parole after service of a minimum period of imprisonment of twenty years.

2. The provisions of this subdivision shall apply in any case where a person is under one or more of the following sentences imposed pursuant to the penal law in effect prior to September first, two thousand seven:

(a) A minimum term of twenty years or more and a maximum of natural life for the crime of murder in the second degree pursuant to section ten hundred forty-eight of such law;
(b) A minimum term of twenty years or more and a maximim of natural life for the crime of kidnapping imposed pursuant to section twelve hundred fifty of such law;
(c) A minimum term of fifteen years or more and a maximum of natural life for a third conviction of a felony under laws relating to narcotic drugs pursuant to section nineteen hundred forty-one of such law; or

(d) A minimum term of fifteen years or more and a maximum of natural life for a fourth conviction of a felony pursuant to section nineteen hundred forty-two of such law.

Any such person who is not otherwise or who will not sooner become eligible for release on parole under such sentence shall be or become eligible for release on parole after service of a minimum period of imprisonment of fifteen years.

3. The provisions of this subdivision shall apply in any case where a person is under a sentence imposed pursuant to the penal law in effect prior to September first, two thousand seven, other than a sentence specified in subdivisions one and two of this section.
Any person who is not otherwise or who will not sooner become eligible for release on parole shall be or become eligible for release on parole under such sentence after service of a minimum period of imprisonment of eight years and four months.

4. In calculating time required to be served prior to eligibility for parole under the minimum periods of imprisonment established by this section, the following rules shall apply:

(a) Service of such time shall be deemed to have commenced on the day the inmate was received in an institution under the jurisdiction of the department pursuant to the sentence;

(b) Where an inmate is under more than one sentence, (i) if the sentences run concurrently, the time served under imprisonment on any of the sentences shall be credited against the minimum periods of all the concurrent sentences, and (ii) if the sentences run consecutively, the minimum periods of imprisonment shall merge in and be satisfied by service of the period that has the longest unexpired time to run;

(c) No credit shall be allowed for *good conduct and efficient and willing performance of duties,* under former section two hundred thirty of this chapter, repealed by chapter four hundred seventy-six of the laws of nineteen hundred seventy and continued in effect as to certain inmates, or under any other provision of law;

(d) Calculations with respect to *jail time, time served under vacated sentence,* and interruption for *escape* shall be in accordance with the provisions of subdivisions three, five, and six of section 70.30 of the penal law as enacted by chapter ten hundred thirty of the laws of nineteen hundred sixty-five, as amended.

5. The provisions of this section shall not be construed as diminishing the discretionary authority of the board of parole to determine whether or not an inmate is to be paroled. The board of parole shall establish special rules for the appearance before the board of those inmates who are or become eligible for parole by virtue of this section on the effective date of the section or within six months after such date, and no such inmate shall have the right to require the board to make a determination prior to the expiration of six months from the date he becomes eligible under this section.

§ 213. Reasons for release

Discretionary release on parole shall not be granted merely as a reward for good conduct or efficient performance of duties assigned in prison, but only if the board of parole is of opinion that there is reasonable probability that, if such prisoner is released, he will live and remain at liberty without violating the law, and that his release is not incompatible with the welfare of society. If the board of parole shall so determine, such prisoner shall be allowed to go upon parole outside of prison walls and enclosure upon such terms and conditions as the board shall prescribe and shall remain while thus on parole in the legal custody of the board of parole until the expiration of the maximum term or period of the sentence or return to an institution under the jurisdiction of the commissioner of correction.

§ 214. Method of release

* * * * *

4. In addition and with respect to all prisoners, the board of parole shall have before it a report from a warden of each prison in which such prisoner has been confined as to the prisoner's conduct in prison, with a detailed statement as to all infractions of prison rules and discipline, all punishments meted out to such prisoner and the circumstances connected therewith, as well as a report from each such warden as to the extent to which such prisoner has responded to the efforts made in prison to improve his mental and moral condition, with a statement as to the prisoner's then attitude towards society, towards the judge who sentenced him, towards the district attorney who prosecuted him, towards the policeman who arrested him, and how the prisoner then regards the crime for which he is in prison and his previous criminal career. In addition, the board shall have before it a report from the superintendent of prison industries giving the prisoner's industrial record while in prison, the average number of hours per day that he has been employed in industry, the nature of his occupations while in prison and a recommendation as to the kind of work he is best fitted to perform and at which he is most likely to succeed when he leaves prison. Such board shall also have before it the report of such physical, mental, and psychiatric examinations as have been made of such prisoner which so far as practicable shall have been made within two months of the time of his eligibility for parole. The board of parole, before releasing any prisoner on parole, shall have the prisoner appear before such board and shall personally examine him and check up so far as possible the reports made by prison wardens and others mentioned in this section. Such board shall reach its own conclusions as to the desirability of releasing such prisoner on parole. No prisoner shall be released on parole unless the board is satisfied that he will be suitably employed in self-sustaining employment is so released.

4. Appearance before the board pursuant to subdivision four of this section shall mean a personal interview by at least three members of the board at the institution in which the inmate is confined or at such other place within the state as may be agreed upon between the chairman of the board and the commissioner of correctional services. Release on parole shall be determined by unanimous vote of the board members who personally interviewed the inmate or by the vote of a majority of the entire board of parole pursuant to rules of the board.

§ 215. Conditions of parole

The board of parole in releasing an inmate on parole shall specify in writing the conditions of his parole, and a copy of such conditions shall be given to the parolee. A violation of such conditions may render the parolee liable to arrest and re-imprisonment. The board shall adopt general rules with regard to conditions of parole and their violation and three members of the board may make special rules to govern particular cases. Such rules, both general and special, may include, among other things, a requirement that the parolee shall not leave the state without the consent of the board, that he shall, if eligible, reside in a suitable hostel or foster home, or that he shall, if eligible, reside in any suitable correctional facility, that he shall contribute to his own support in such hostel, foster home, or correctional facility, that he shall contribute to the support of his dependents, that he shall make restitution for his crime, that he shall, if there is a record, report or other evidence satisfactory to the board that he is addicted to the use of narcotic drugs, take clinic or similar treatment for narcotic addiction at a hospital or other facility where such treatment is available, that he shall abandon evil associates and ways, that he shall carry out the instructions of his parole officer and, in general, so comport himself as such officers shall determine.

KEY (CORRECT ANSWERS)

1. C
2. C
3. B
4. C
5. D

6. D
7. A
8. A
9. B
10. D

11. B
12. B
13. A
14. D
15. C

16. A
17. B
18. C
19. A
20. D

———

PREPARING WRITTEN MATERIAL
EXAMINATION SECTION
TEST 1

DIRECTIONS: Each question or incomplete statement is followed by several suggested answers or completions. Select the one that BEST answers the question or completes the statement. *PRINT THE LETTER OF THE CORRECT ANSWER IN THE SPACE AT THE RIGHT.*

1. The one of the following sentences which is LEAST acceptable from the viewpoint of correct usage is:
   A. The police thought the fugitive to be him.
   B. The criminals set a trap for whoever would fall into it.
   C. It is ten years ago since the fugitive fled from the city.
   D. The lecturer argued that criminals are usually cowards.
   E. The police removed four bucketfuls of earth from the scene of the crime.

1.____

2. The one of the following sentences which is LEAST acceptable from the viewpoint of correct usage is:
   A. The patrolman scrutinized the report with great care.
   B. Approaching the victim of the assault, two bruises were noticed by the patrolman.
   C. As soon as I had broken down the door, I stepped into the room.
   D. I observed the accused loitering near the building, which was closed at the time.
   E. The storekeeper complained that his neighbor was guilty of violating a local ordinance.

2.____

3. The one of the following sentences which is LEAST acceptable from the viewpoint of correct usage is:
   A. I realized immediately that he intended to assault the woman, so I disarmed him.
   B. It was apparent that Mr. Smith's explanation contained many inconsistencies.
   C. Despite the slippery condition of the street, he managed to stop the vehicle before injuring the child.
   D. Not a single one of them wish, despite the damage to property, to make a formal complaint.
   E. The body was found lying on the floor.

3.____

4. The one of the following sentences which contains NO error in usage is:
   A. After the robbers left, the proprietor stood tied in his chair for about two hours before help arrived.
   B. In the cellar I found the watchman's hat and coat.
   C. The persons living in adjacent apartments stated that they had heard no unusual noises.

4.____

D. Neither a knife or any firearms were found in the room.
E. Walking down the street, the shouting of the crowd indicated that something was wrong.

5. The one of the following sentences which contains NO error in usage is:
   A. The policeman lay a firm hand on the suspect's shoulder.
   B. It is true that neither strength nor agility are the most important requirement for a good patrolman.
   C. Good citizens constantly strive to do more than merely comply the restraints imposed by society.
   D. No decision was made as to whom the prize should be awarded.
   E. Twenty years is considered a severe sentence for a felony.

6. Which of the following sentences is NOT expressed in standard English usage?
   A. The victim reached a pay-phone booth and manages to call police headquarters.
   B. By the time the call was received, the assailant had left the scene.
   C. The victim has been a respected member of the community for the past eleven years.
   D. Although the lighting was bad and the shadows were deep, the storekeeper caught sight of the attacker.
   E. Additional street lights have since been installed, and the patrols have been strengthened.

7. Which of the following sentences is NOT expressed in standard English usage?
   A. The judge upheld the attorney's right to question the witness about the missing glove.
   B. To be absolutely fair to all parties is the jury's chief responsibility.
   C. Having finished the report, a loud noise in the next room startled the sergeant.
   D. The witness obviously enjoyed having played a part in the proceedings.
   E. The sergeant planned to assign the case to whoever arrived first.

8. In which of the following sentences is a word misused?
   A. As a matter of principle, the captain insisted that the suspect's partner be brought for questioning.
   B. The principle suspect had been detained at the station house for most of the day.
   C. The principal in the crime had no previous criminal record, but his closest associate had been convicted of felonies on two occasions.
   D. The interest payments had been made promptly, but the firm had been drawing upon the principal for these payments.
   E. The accused insisted that his high school principal would furnish him a character reference.

9. Which of the following statements is ambiguous? 9.____
   A. Mr. Sullivan explained why Mr. Johnson had been dismissed from his job.
   B. The storekeeper told the patrolman he had made a mistake.
   C. After waiting three hours, the patients in the doctor's office were sent home.
   D. The janitor's duties were to maintain the building in good shape and to answer tenants' complaints.
   E. The speed limit should, in my opinion, be raised to sixty miles an hour on that stretch of road.

10. In which of the following is the punctuation or capitalization faulty? 10.____
    A. The accident occurred at an intersection in the Kew Gardens section of Queens, near the bus stop.
    B. The sedan, not the convertible, was struck in the side.
    C. Before any of the patrolmen had left the police car received an important message from headquarters.
    D. The dog that had been stolen was returned to his master, John Dempsey, who lived in East Village.
    E. The letter had been sent to 12 Hillside Terrace, Rutland, Vermont 05702.

Questions 11-25.

DIRECTIONS: Questions 11 through 25 are to be answered in accordance with correct English usage; that is, standard English rather than nonstandard or substandard. Nonstandard and substandard English includes words or expressions usually classified as slang, dialect, illiterate, etc., which are not generally accepted as correct in current written communication. Standard English also requires clarity, proper punctuation and capitalization and appropriate use of words. Write the letter of the sentence NOT expressed in standard English usage in the space at the right.

11. A. There were three witnesses to the accident. 11.____
    B. At least three witnesses were found to testify for the plaintiff.
    C. Three of the witnesses who took the stand was uncertain about the defendant's competence to drive.
    D. Only three witnesses came forward to testify for the plaintiff.
    E. The three witnesses to the accident were pedestrians.

12. A. The driver had obviously drunk too many martinis before leaving for home. 12.____
    B. The boy who drowned had swum in these same waters many times before.
    C. The petty thief had stolen a bicycle from a private driveway before he was apprehended.
    D. The detectives had brung in the heroin shipment they intercepted.
    E. The passengers had never ridden in a converted bus before.

13. A. Between you and me, the new platoon plan sounds like a good idea.
    B. Money from an aunt's estate was left to his wife and he.
    C. He and I were assigned to the same patrol for the first time in two months.
    D. Either you or he should check the front door of that store.
    E. The captain himself was not sure of the witness's reliability.

    13._____

14. A. The alarm had scarcely begun to ring when the explosion occurred.
    B. Before the firemen arrived at the scene, the second story had been destroyed.
    C. Because of the dense smoke and heat, the firemen could hardly approach the now-blazing structure.
    D. According to the patrolman's report, there wasn't nobody in the store when the explosion occurred.
    E. The sergeant's suggestion was not at all unsound, but no one agreed with him.

    14._____

15. A. The driver and the passenger they were both found to be intoxicated.
    B. The driver and the passenger talked slowly and not too clearly.
    C. Neither the driver nor his passengers were able to give a coherent account of the accident.
    D. In a corner of the room sat the passenger, quietly dozing.
    E. the driver finally told a strange and unbelievable story, which the passenger contradicted.

    15._____

16. A. Under the circumstances I decided not to continue my examination of the premises.
    B. There are many difficulties now not comparable with those existing in 1960.
    C. Friends of the accused were heard to announce that the witness had better been away on the day of the trial.
    D. The two criminals escaped in the confusion that followed the explosion.
    E. The aged man was struck by the considerateness of the patrolman's offer.

    16._____

17. A. An assemblage of miscellaneous weapons lay on the table.
    B. Ample opportunities were given to the defendant to obtain counsel.
    C. The speaker often alluded to his past experience with youthful offenders in the armed forces.
    D. The sudden appearance of the truck aroused my suspicions.
    E. Her studying had a good affect on her grades in high school.

    17._____

18. A. He sat down in the theater and began to watch the movie.
    B. The girl had ridden horses since she was four years old.
    C. Application was made on behalf of the prosecutor to cite the witness for contempt.
    D. The bank robber, with his two accomplices, were caught in the act.
    E. His story is simply not credible.

    18._____

19. A. The angry boy said that he did not like those kind of friends.
    B. The merchant's financial condition was so precarious that he felt he must avail himself of any offer of assistance.
    C. He is apt to promise more than he can perform.
    D. Looking at the messy kitchen, the housewife felt like crying.
    E. A clerk was left in charge of the stolen property.

20. A. His wounds were aggravated by prolonged exposure to sub-freezing temperatures.
    B. The prosecutor remarked that the witness was not averse to changing his story each time he was interviewed.
    C. The crime pattern indicated that the burglars were adapt in the handling of explosives.
    D. His rigid adherence to a fixed plan brought him into renewed conflict with his subordinates.
    E. He had anticipated that the sentence would be delivered by noon.

21. A. The whole arraignment procedure is badly in need of revision.
    B. After his glasses were broken in the fight, he would of gone to the optometrist if he could.
    C. Neither Tom nor Jack brought his lunch to work.
    D. He stood aside until the quarrel was over.
    E. A statement in the psychiatrist's report disclosed that the probationer vowed to have his revenge.

22. A. His fiery and intemperate speech to the striking employees fatally affected any chance of a future reconciliation.
    B. The wording of the statute has been variously construed.
    C. The defendant's attorney, speaking in the courtroom, called the official a demagogue who contempuously disregarded the judge's orders.
    D. The baseball game is likely to be the most exciting one this year.
    E. The mother divided the cookies among her two children.

23. A. There was only a bed and a dresser in the dingy room.
    B. John was one of the few students that have protested the new rule.
    C. It cannot be argued that the child's testimony is negligible; it is, on the contrary, of the greatest importance.
    D. The basic criterion for clearance was so general that officials resolved any doubts in favor of dismissal.
    E. Having just returned from a long vacation, the officer found the city unbearably hot.

24. A. The librarian ought to give more help to small children.
    B. The small boy was criticized by the teacher because he often wrote careless.
    C. It was generally doubted whether the women would permit the use of her apartment for intelligence operations.
    D. The probationer acts differently every time the officer visits him.
    E. Each of the newly appointed officers has 12 years of service.

25. A. The North is the most industrialized region in the country.
    B. L. Patrick Gray 3d, the bureau's acting director, stated that, while "rehabilitation is fine" for some convicted criminals, "it is a useless gesture for those who resist every such effort."
    C. Careless driving, faulty mechanism, narrow or badly kept roads all play their part in causing accidents.
    D. The childrens' books were left in the bus.
    E. It was a matter of internal security; consequently, he felt no inclination to rescind his previous order.

25.____

KEY (CORRECT ANSWERS)

1.	C		11.	C
2.	B		12.	D
3.	D		13.	B
4.	C		14.	D
5.	E		15.	A
6.	A		16.	C
7.	C		17.	E
8.	B		18.	D
9.	B		19.	A
10.	C		20.	C

21.	B
22.	E
23.	B
24.	B
25.	D

TEST 2

DIRECTIONS: Each question or incomplete statement is followed by several suggested answers or completions. Select the one that BEST answers the question or completes the statement. *PRINT THE LETTER OF THE CORRECT ANSWER IN THE SPACE AT THE RIGHT.*

Questions 1-6.

DIRECTIONS: Each of Questions 1 through 6 consists of a statement which contains a word (one of those underlined) that is either incorrectly used because it is not in keeping with the meaning the quotation is evidently intended to convey, or is misspelled. There is only one INCORRECT word in each quotation. Of the four underlined words, determine if the first one should be replaced by the word lettered A, the second replaced by the word lettered B, the third replaced by the word lettered C, or the fourth replaced by the word lettered D.

1. Whether one depends on fluorescent or artificial light or both, adequate standards should be maintained by means of systematic tests. 1.____
   A. natural   B. safeguards   C. established   D. routine

2. A police officer has to be prepared to assume his knowledge as a social scientist in the community. 2.____
   A. forced   B. role   C. philosopher   D. street

3. It is practically impossible to indicate whether a sentence is too long simply by measuring its length. 3.____
   A. almost   B. tell   C. very   D. guessing

4. Strong leaders are required to organize a community for delinquency prevention and for dissemination of organized crime and drug addiction. 4.____
   A. tactics   B. important   C. control   D. meetings

5. The demonstrators who were taken to the Criminal Courts building in Manhattan (because it was large enough to accommodate them), contended that the arrests were unwarranted. 5.____
   A. demonstraters   B. Manhatten
   C. accomodate   D. unwarranted

6. They were guaranteed a calm atmosphere, free from harassment, which would be conducive to quiet consideration of the indictments. 6.____
   A. guarenteed   B. atmspher
   C. harassment   D. inditements

Questions 7-11.

DIRECTIONS: Each of Questions 7 through 11 consists of a statement containing four words in capital letters. One of these words in capital letters is not in keeping with the meaning which the statement is evidently intended to carry. The four words in capital letters in each statement are reprinted after the statement. Print the capital letter preceding the one of the four words which does MOST to spoil the true meaning of the statement in the space at the right.

7. Retirement and pension systems are essential not only to provide employees with with a means of support in the future, but also to prevent longevity and CHARITABLE considerations from UPSETTING the PROMOTIONAL opportunities RETIRED members of the career service. 7.____
    A. charitable   B. upsetting   C. promotional   D. retired

8. Within each major DIVISION in a properly set up public or private organization, provision is made so that each NECESSARY activity is CARED for and lines of authority and responsibility are clear-cut and INFINITE. 8.____
    A. division   B. necessary   C. cared   D. infinite

9. In public service, the scale of salaries paid must be INCIDENTAL to the services rendered, with due CONSIDERATION for the attraction of the desired MANPOWER and for the maintenance of a standard of living COMMENSURATE with the work to be performed. 9.____
    A. incidental   B. consideration
    C. manpower   D. commensurate

10. An understanding of the AIMS of an organization by the staff will AID greatly in increasing the DEMAND of the correspondence work of the office, and will to a large extent DETERMINE the nature of the correspondence. 10.____
    A. aims   B. aid   C. demand   D. determine

11. BECAUSE the Civil Service Commission strongly feels that the MERIT system is a key factor in the MAINTENANCE of democratic government, it has adopted as one of its major DEFENSES the progressive democratization of its own procedures in dealing with candidates for positions in the public service. 11.____
    A. Because   B. merit   C. maintenance   D. defenses

Questions 12-14.

DIRECTIONS: Questions 12 through 14 consist of one sentence each. Each sentence contains an incorrectly used word. First, decide which is the incorrectly used word. Then, from among the options given, decide which word, when substituted for the incorrectly used word, makes the meaning of the sentence clear.
EXAMPLE:
The U.S. national income exhibits a pattern of long term deflection.
    A. reflection   B. subjection   C. rejoicing   D. growth

The word *deflection* in the sentence does not convey the meaning the sentence evidently intended to convey. The word *growth* (Answer D), when substituted for the word *deflection*, makes the meaning of the sentence clear. Accordingly, the answer to the question is D.

12. The study commissioned by the joint committee fell compassionately short of the mark and would have to be redone.
    A. successfully   B. insignificantly
    C. experimentally   D. woefully

13. He will not idly exploit any violation of the provisions of the order.
    A. tolerate   B. refuse   C. construe   D. guard

14. The defendant refused to be virile and bitterly protested service.
    A. irked   B. feasible   C. docile   D. credible

Questions 15-25.

DIRECTIONS: Questions 15 through 25 consist of short paragraphs. Each paragraph contains one word which is INCORRECTLY used because it is NOT in keeping with the meaning of the paragraph. Find the word in each paragraph which is INCORRECTLY used and then select as the answer the suggested word which should be substituted for the incorrectly used word.

SAMPLE QUESTION:
In determining who is to do the work in your unit, you will have to decide just who does what from day to day. One of your lowest responsibilities is to assign work so that everybody gets a fair share and that everyone can do his part well.
    A. new   B. old   C. important   D. performance

EXPLANATION:
The word which is NOT in keeping with the meaning of the paragraph is *lowest*. This is the INCORRECTLY used word. The suggested word *important* would be in keeping with the meaning of the paragraph and should be substituted for *lowest*. Therefore, the CORRECT answer is choice C.

15. If really good practice in the elimination of preventable injuries is to be achieved and held in any establishment, top management must refuse full and definite responsibility and must apply a good share of its attention to the task.
    A. accept   B. avoidable   C. duties   D. problem

16. Recording the human face for identification is by no means the only service performed by the camera in the field of investigation. When the trial of any issue takes place, a word picture is sought to be distorted to the court of incidents, occurrences, or events which are in dispute.
    A. appeals   B. description   C. portrayed   D. deranged

17. In the collection of physical evidence, it cannot be emphasized too strongly that a haphazard systematic search at the scene of the crime is vital. Nothing must be overlooked. Often the only leads in a case will come from the results of this search.
    A. important	B. investigation
    C. proof	D. thorough

17.____

18. If an investigator has reason to suspect that the witness is mentally stable, or a habitual drunkard, he should leave no stone unturned in his investigation to determine if the witness was under the influence of liquor or drugs, or was mentally unbalanced either at the time of the occurrence to which he testified or at the time of the trial.
    A. accused	B. clue	C. deranged	D. question

18.____

19. The use of records is a valuable step in crime investigation and is the main reason every department should maintain accurate reports. Crimes are not committed through the use of departmental records alone but from the use of all records, of almost every type, wherever they may be found and whenever they give any incidental information regarding the criminal.
    A. accidental	B. necessary	C. reported	D. solved

19.____

20. In the years since passage of the Harrison Narcotic Act of 1914, making the possession of opium amphetamines illegal in most circumstances, drug use has become a subject of considerable scientific interest and investigation. There is at present a voluminous literature on drug use of various kinds.
    A. ingestion	B. derivatives	C. addiction	D. opiates

20.____

21. Of course, the fact that criminal laws are extremely patterned in definition does not mean that the majority of persons who violate them are dealt with as criminals. Quite the contrary, for a great many forbidden acts are voluntarily engaged in within situations of privacy and go unobserved and unreported.
    A. symbolic	B. casual	C. scientific	D. broad-gauged

21.____

22. The most punitive way to study punishment is to focus attention on the pattern of punitive action: to study how a penalty is applied, too study what is done to or taken from an offender.
    A. characteristic	B. degrading	C. objective	D. distinguished

22.____

23. The most common forms of punishment in times past have been death, physical torture, mutilation, branding, public humiliation, fines, forfeits of property, banishment, transportation, and imprisonment. Although this list is by no means differentiated, practically every form of punishment has had several variations and applications.
    A. specific	B. simple	C. exhaustive	D. characteristic

23.____

24. There is another important line of inference between ordinary and professional criminals, and that is the source from which they are recruited. The professional criminal seems to be drawn from legitimate employment and, in many instances, from parallel vocations or pursuits.
    A. demarcation   B. justification   C. superiority   D. reference

24.____

25. He took the position that the success of the program was insidious on getting additional revenue.
    A. reputed   B. contingent   C. failure   D. indeterminate

25.____

KEY (CORRECT ANSWERS)

1.	A	11.	D
2.	B	12.	D
3.	B	13.	A
4.	C	14.	C
5.	D	15.	A
6.	C	16.	C
7.	D	17.	D
8.	D	18.	C
9.	A	19.	D
10.	C	20.	B

21.	D
22.	C
23.	C
24.	A
25.	B

TEST 3

DIRECTIONS: Each question or incomplete statement is followed by several suggested answers or completions. Select the one that BEST answers the question or completes the statement. *PRINT THE LETTER OF THE CORRECT ANSWER IN THE SPACE AT THE RIGHT.*

Questions 1-5.

DIRECTIONS: Questions 1 through 5 are to be answered on the basis of the following.

You are a supervising officer in an investigative unit. Earlier in the day, you directed Detectives Tom Dixon and Sal Mayo to investigate a reported assault and robbery in a liquor store within your area of jurisdiction.

Detective Dixon has submitted to you a preliminary investigative report containing the following information:

- At 1630 hours on 2/20, arrived at Joe's Liquor Store at 350 SW Avenue with Detective Mayo to investigate A & R.
- At store interviewed Rob Ladd, store manager, who stated that he and Joe Brown (store owner) had been stuck up about ten minutes prior to our arrival.
- Ladd described the robbers as male whites in their late teens or early twenties. Further stated that one of the robbers displayed what appeared to be an automatic pistol as he entered the store, and said, *Give us the money or we'll kill you*. Ladd stated that Brown then reached under the counter where he kept a loaded .38 caliber pistol. Several shots followed, and Ladd threw himself to the floor.
- The robbers fled, and Ladd didn't know if any money had been taken.
- At this point, Ladd realized that Brown was unconscious on the floor and bleeding from a head wound.
- Ambulance called by Ladd, and Brown was removed by same to General Hospital.
- Personally interviewed John White, 382 Dartmouth Place, who stated he was inside store at the time of occurrence. White states that he hid behind a wine display upon hearing someone say, *Give us the money*. He then heard shots and saw two young men run from the store to a yellow car parked at the curb. White was unable to further describe auto. States the taller of the two men drove the car away while the other sat on passenger side in front.
- Recovered three spent .38 caliber bullets from premises and delivered them to Crime Lab.
- To General Hospital at 1800 hours but unable to interview Brown, who was under sedation and suffering from shock and a laceration of the head.
- Alarm #12487 transmitted for car and occupants.
- Case Active.

Based solely on the contents of the preliminary investigation submitted by Detective Dixon, select one sentence from the following groups of sentences which is MOST accurate and is grammatically correct.

1. A. Both robbers were armed.
    B. Each of the robbers were described as a male white.
    C. Neither robber was armed.
    D. Mr. Ladd stated that one of the robbers was armed.

    1._____

2. A. Mr. Brown fired three shots from his revolver.
    B. Mr. Brown was shot in the head by one of the robbers.
    C. Mr. Brown suffered a gunshot wound of the head during the course of the robbery.
    D. Mr. Brown was taken to General Hospital by ambulance.

    2._____

3. A. Shots were fired after one of the robbers said, *Give us the money or we'll kill you.*
    B. After one of the robbers demanded the money from Mr. Brown, he fired a shot.
    C. The preliminary investigation indicated that although Mr. Brown did not have a license for the gun, he was justified in using deadly physical force.
    D. Mr. Brown was interviewed at General Hospital.

    3._____

4. A. Each of the witnesses were customers in the store at the time of occurrence.
    B. Neither of the witnesses interviewed was the owner of the liquor store.
    C. Neither of the witnesses interviewed were the owner of the store.
    D. Neither of the witnesses was employed by Mr. Brown.

    4._____

5. A. Mr. Brown arrived at General Hospital at about 5:00 P.M.
    B. Neither of the robbers was injured during the robbery.
    C. The robbery occurred at 3:30 P.M. on February 10.
    D. One of the witnesses called the ambulance.

    5._____

Questions 6-10.

DIRECTIONS: Each of Questions 6 through 10 consists of information given in outline form and four sentences labeled A, B, C, and D. For each question, choose the one sentence which CORRECTLY expresses the information given in outline form and which also displays PROPER English usage.

6. Client's Name: Joanna Jones
    Number of Children: 3
    Client's Income: None
    Client's Marital Status: Single

    6._____

    A. Joanna Jones is an unmarried client with three children who have no income.
    B. Joanna Jones, who is single and has no income, a client she has three children.
    C. Joanna Jones, whose three children are clients, is single and has no income.
    D. Joanna Jones, who has three children, is an unmarried client with no income.

7. Client's Name: Bertha Smith
   Number of Children: 2
   Client's Rent: $1050 per month
   Number of Rooms: 4

   A. Bertha Smith, a client, pays $1050 per month for her four rooms with two children.
   B. Client Bertha Smith has two children and pays $1050 per month for four rooms.
   C. Client Bertha Smith is paying $1050 per month for two children with four rooms.
   D. For four rooms and two children client Bertha Smith pays $1050 per month.

7.____

8. Name of Employee: Cynthia Dawes
   Number of Cases Assigned: 9
   Date Cases were Assigned: 12/16
   Number of Assigned Cases Completed: 8

   A. On December 16, employee Cynthia Dawes was assigned nine cases; she has completed eight of these cases.
   B. Cynthia Dawes, employee on December 16, assigned nine cases, completed eight.
   C. Being employed on December 16, Cynthia Dawes completed eight of nine assigned cases.
   D. Employee Cynthia Dawes, she was assigned nine cases and completed eight, on December 16.

8.____

9. Place of Audit: Broadway Center
   Names of Auditors: Paul Cahn, Raymond Perez
   Date of Audit: 11/20
   Number of Cases Audited: 41

   A. On November 20, at the Broadway Center 41 cases was audited by auditors Paul Cahn and Raymond Perez.
   B. Auditors Raymond Perez and Paul Cahn has audited 41 cases at the Broadway Center on November 20.
   C. At the Broadway Center, on November 20, auditors Paul Cahn and Raymond Perez audited 41 cases.
   D. Auditors Paul Cahn and Raymond Perez at the Broadway Center, on November 20, is auditing 41 cases.

9.____

10. Name of Client: Barbra Levine
    Client's Monthly Income: $2100
    Client's Monthly Expenses: $4520

    A. Barbra Levine is a client, her monthly income is $2100 and her monthly expenses is $4520.
    B. Barbra Levine's monthly income is $2100 and she is a client, with whose monthly expenses are $4520.

10.____

C. Barbra Levine is a client whose monthly income is $2100 and whose monthly expenses are $4520.
D. Barbra Levine, a client, is with a monthly income which is $2100 and monthly expenses which are $4520.

Questions 11-13.

DIRECTIONS: Questions 11 through 13 involve several statements of fact presented in a very simple way. These statements of fact are followed by 4 choices which attempt to incorporate all of the facts into one logical statement which is properly constructed and grammatically correct.

11. I. Mr. Brown was sweeping the sidewalk in front of his house. 11._____
    II. He was sweeping it because it was dirty.
    III. He swept the refuse into the street.
    IV. Police Officer gave him a ticket.

   Which one of the following BEST presents the information given above?
   A. Because his sidewalk was dirty, Mr. Brown received a ticket from Officer Green when he swept the refuse into the street.
   B. Police Officer Green gave Mr. Brown a ticket because his sidewalk was dirty and he swept the refuse into the street.
   C. Police Officer Green gave Mr. Brown a ticket for sweeping refuse into the street because his sidewalk was dirty.
   D. Mr. Brown, who was sweeping refuse from his dirty sidewalk into the street, was given a ticket by Police Officer Green.

12. I. Sergeant Smith radioed for help. 12._____
    II. The sergeant did so because the crowd was getting larger.
    III. It was 10:00 A.M. when he made his call.
    IV. Sergeant Smith was not in uniform at the time of occurrence.

   Which one of the following BEST presents the information given above?
   A. Sergeant Smith, although not on duty at the time, radioed for help at 10 o'clock because the crowd was getting uglier.
   B. Although not in uniform, Sergeant Smith called for help at 10:00 A.M. because the crowd was getting uglier.
   C. Sergeant Smith radioed for help at 10:00 A.M. because the crowd was getting larger.
   D. Although he was not in uniform, Sergeant Smith radioed for help at 10:00 A.M. because the crowd was getting larger.

13. I. The payroll office is open on Fridays. 13._____
    II. Paychecks are distributed from 9:00 A.M. to 12 Noon.
    III. The office is open on Fridays because that's the only day the payroll staff is available.
    IV. It is open for the specified hours in order to permit employees to cash checks at the bank during lunch hour.

The choice below which MOST clearly and accurately presents the above idea is:

A. Because the payroll office is open on Fridays from 9:00 A.M. to 12 Noon, employees can cash their checks when the payroll staff is available.
B. Because the payroll staff is only available on Fridays until noon, employees can cash their checks during their lunch hour.
C. Because the payroll staff is available only on Fridays, the office is open from 9:00 A.M. to 12 Noon to allow employees to cash their checks.
D. Because of payroll staff availability, the payroll office is open on Fridays. It is open from 9:00 A.M. to 12 Noon so that distributed paychecks can be cashed at the bank while employees are on their lunch hour.

Questions 14-16.

DIRECTIONS: In each of Questions 14 through 6, the four sentences are from a paragraph in a report. They are not in the right order. Which of the following arrangements is the BEST one?

14. I. An executive may answer a letter by writing his reply on the face of the letter itself instead of having a return letter typed.
    II. This procedure is efficient because it saves the executive's time, the typist's time, and saves office file space.
    III. Copying machines are used in small offices as well as large offices to save time and money in making brief replies to business letters.
    IV. A copy is made on a copy machine to go into the company files, while the original is mailed back to the sender.

    The CORRECT answer is:
    A. I, II, IV, III   B. I, IV, II, III   C. III, I, IV, II   D. III, IV, II, I

14.____

15. I. Most organizations favor one of the types but always include the others to a lesser degree.
    II. However, we can detect a definite trend toward greater use of symbolic control.
    III. We suggest that our local police agencies are today primarily utilizing material control.
    IV. Control can be classified into three types: physical, material, and symbolic.

    The CORRECT answer is:
    A. IV, II, III, I   B. II, I, IV, III   C. III, IV, II, I   D. IV, I, III, II

15.____

16. I. They can and do take advantage of ancient political and geographical boundaries, which often give them sanctuary from effective policy activity.
    II. This country is essentially a country of small police forces, each operating independently within the limits of its jurisdiction.
    III. The boundaries that define and limit police operations do not hinder the movement of criminals, of course.
    IV. The machinery of law enforcement in America is fragmented, complicated, and frequently overlapping.

16.____

The CORRECT answer is:
A. III, I, IV   B. II, IV, I, III   C. IV, II, III, I   D. IV, III, II, I

17. Examine the following sentence, and then choose from below the words which should be inserted in the blank spaces to produce the best sentence.
The unit has exceeded _____ goals and the employees are satisfied with _____ accomplishments.
A. their, it's   B. it's; it's   C. its, there   D. its, their

17.____

18. Examine the following sentence, and then choose from below the words which should be inserted in the blank spaces to produce the best sentence.
Research indicates that employees who _____ no opportunity for close social relationships often find their work unsatisfying, and this _____ of satisfaction often reflects itself in low production.
A. have; lack   B. have; excess   C. has; lack   D. has; excess

18.____

19. Words in a sentence must be arranged properly to make sure that the intended meaning of the sentence is clear.
The sentence below that does NOT make sense because a clause has been separated from the word on which its meaning depends is:
A. To be a good writer, clarity is necessary.
B. To be a good writer, you must write clearly.
C. You must write clearly to be a good writer.
D. Clarity is necessary to good writing.

19.____

Questions 20-21.

DIRECTIONS: Each of Questions 20 and 21 consists of a statement which contains a word (one of those underlined) that is either incorrectly used because it is not in keeping with the meaning the quotation is evidently intended to convey, or is misspelled. There is only one INCORRECT word in each quotation. Of the four underlined words, determine if the first one should be replaced by the word lettered A, the second one replaced by the word lettered B, the third one replaced by the word lettered C, or the fourth one replaced by the word lettered D.

20. The alleged killer was occasionally permitted to excercise in the corridor.
A. alledged   B. ocasionally   C. permited   D. exercise

20.____

21. Defense counsel stated, in affect, that their conduct was permissible under the First Amendment.
A. council   B. effect   C. there   D. permissable

21.____

Question 22.

DIRECTIONS: Question 22 consists of one sentence. This sentence contains an incorrectly used word. First, decide which is the incorrectly used word. Then, from among the options given, decide which word, when substituted for the incorrectly used word, makes the meaning of the sentence clear.

22. As today's violence has no single cause, so its causes have no single scheme. 22.____
    A. deference   B. cure   C. flaw   D. relevance

23. In the sentence, *A man in a light-grey suit waited thirty-five minutes in the ante-room for the all-important document*, the word IMPROPERLY hyphenated is 23.____
    A. light-grey   B. thirty-five
    C. ante-room   D. all-important

24. In the sentence, *The candidate wants to file his application for preference before it is too late*, the word *before* is used as a(n) 24.____
    A. preposition   B. subordinating conjunction
    C. pronoun   D. adverb

25. In the sentence, *The perpetrators ran from the scene*, the word *from* is a 25.____
    A. preposition   B. pronoun   C. verb   D. conjunction

KEY (CORRECT ANSWERS)

1.	D		11.	D
2.	D		12.	D
3.	A		13.	D
4.	B		14.	C
5.	D		15.	D
6.	D		16.	C
7.	B		17.	D
8.	A		18.	A
9.	C		19.	A
10.	C		20.	D

21.	B
22.	B
23.	C
24.	B
25.	A

PREPARING WRITTEN MATERIAL

PARAGRAPH REARRANGEMENT
COMMENTARY

The sentences that follow are in scrambled order. You are to rearrange them in proper order and indicate the letter choice containing the correct answer at the space at the right.

Each group of sentences in this section is actually a paragraph presented in scrambled order. Each sentence in the group has a place in that paragraph; no sentence is to be left out. You are to read each group of sentences and decide upon the best order in which to put the sentences so as to form a well-organized paragraph.

The questions in this section measure the ability to solve a problem when all the facts relevant to its solution are not given.

More specifically, certain positions of responsibility and authority require the employee to discover connection between events sometimes, apparently, unrelated. In order to do this, the employee will find it necessary to correctly infer that unspecified events have probably occurred or are likely to occur. This ability becomes especially important when action must be taken on incomplete information.

Accordingly, these questions require competitors to choose among several suggested alternatives, each of which presents a different sequential arrangement of the events. Competitors must choose the MOST logical of the suggested sequences.

In order to do so, they may be required to draw on general knowledge to infer missing concepts or events that are essential to sequencing the given events. Competitors should be careful to infer only what is essential to the sequence. The plausibility of the wrong alternatives will always require the inclusion of unlikely events or of additional chains of events which are NOT essential to sequencing the given events.

It's very important to remember that you are looking for the best of the four possible choices, and that the best choice of all may not even be one of the answers you're given to choose from.

There is no one right way to solve these problems. Many people have found it helpful to first write out the order of the sentences, as they would have arranged them, on their scrap paper before looking at the possible answers. If their optimum answer is there, this can save them some time. If it isn't, this method can still give insight into solving the problem. Others find it most helpful to just go through each of the possible choices, contrasting each as they go along. You should use whatever method feels comfortable and works for you.

While most of these types of questions are not that difficult, we've added a higher percentage of the difficult type, just to give you more practice. Usually there are only one or two questions on this section that contain such subtle distinctions that you're unable to answer confidently. And you then may find yourself stuck deciding between two possible choices, neither of which you're sure about.

EXAMINATION SECTION
TEST 1

DIRECTIONS: Each question consists of several sentences which can be arranged in a logical sequence. For each question, select the choice which places the numbered sentences in the MOST logical sequence. *PRINT THE LETTER OF THE CORRECT ANSWER IN THE SPACE AT THE RIGHT.*

1. I. A body was found in the woods.
    II. A man proclaimed innocence.
    III. The owner of a gun was located.
    IV. A gun was traced.
    V. The owner of a gun was questioned.
    The CORRECT answer is:
    A. IV, III, V, II, I B. II, I, IV, III, V C. I, IV, III, V, II
    D. I, III, V, II, IV E. I, II, IV, III, V

    1.____

2. I. A man is in a hunting accident.
    II. A man fell down a flight of steps.
    III. A man lost his vision in one eye,
    IV. A man broke his leg.
    V. A man had to walk with a cane.
    The CORRECT answer is:
    A. II, IV, V, I, III B. IV, V, I, III, II C. III, I, IV, V, II
    D. I, III, V, II, IV E. I, III, II, IV, V

    2.____

3. I. A man is offered a new job.
    II. A woman is offered a new job.
    III. A man works as a waiter.
    IV. A woman works as a waitress.
    V. A woman gives notice.
    The CORRECT answer is:
    A. IV, II, V, III, I B. IV, II, V, I, III C. II, IV, V, III, I
    D. III, I, IV, II, V E. IV, III, II, V, I

    3.____

4. I. A train let the station late.
    II. A man was late for work.
    III. A man lost his job.
    IV. Many people complained because the train was late.
    V. There was a traffic jam.
    The CORRECT answer is:
    A. V, II, I, IV, III B. V, I, IV, II, III C. V, I, II, IV, III
    D. I, V, IV, II, III E. II, I, IV, V, III

    4.____

5. I. The burden of proof as to each issue is determined before trial and remains upon the same party throughout the trial.
    II. The jury is at liberty to believe one witness' testimony as against a number of contradictory witnesses.
    III. In a civil case, the party bearing the burden of proof is required to prove his contention by a fair preponderance of the evidence.
    IV. However, it must be noted that a fair preponderance of evidence does not necessarily mean a greater number of witnesses.
    V. The burden of proof is the burden which rests upon one of the parties to an action to persuade the trier of the facts, generally the jury, that a proposition he asserts is true.
    VI. If the evidence is equally balanced, or if it leaves the jury in such doubt as to be unable to decide the controversy either way, judgment must be given against the party upon whom the burden of proof rests.
    The CORRECT answer is:
    A. III, II, V, IV, I, VI   B. I, II, VI, V, III, IV   C. III, IV, V, I, II, VI
    D. V, I, III, VI, IV, II   E. I, V, III, VI, IV, II

6. I. If a parent is without assets and is unemployed, he cannot be convicted of the crime of non-support of a child.
    II. The term *sufficient ability* has been held to mean sufficient financial ability.
    III. It does not matter if his unemployment is by choice or unavoidable circumstances.
    IV. If he fails to take any steps at all, he may be liable to prosecution for endangering the welfare of a child.
    V. Under the penal law, a parent is responsible for the support of his minor child only if the parent is of *sufficient ability*.
    VI. An indigent parent may meet his obligation by borrowing money or by seeking aid under the provisions of the Social Welfare Law.
    The CORRECT answer is:
    A. VI, I, V, III, II, IV   B. I, III, V, II, IV, VI   C. V, II, I, III, VI, IV
    D. I, VI, IV, V, II, III   E. II, V, I, III, VI, IV

7. I. Consider, for example, the case of a rabble rouser who urges a group of twenty people to go out and break the windows of a nearby factory.
    II. Therefore, the law fills the indicated gap with the crime of *inciting to riot*.
    III. A person is considered guilty of inciting to riot when he urges ten or more persons to engage in tumultuous and violent conduct of a kind likely to create public alarm.
    IV. However, if he has not obtained the cooperation of at least four people, he cannot be charged with unlawful assembly.
    V. The charge of inciting to riot was added to the law to cover types of conduct which cannot be classified as either the crime of *riot* or the crime of *unlawful assembly*.
    VI. If he acquires the acquiescence of at least four of them, he is guilty of unlawful assembly even if the project does not materialize.
    The CORRECT answer is:
    A. III, V, I, VI, IV, II   B. V, I, IV, VI, II, III   C. III, IV, I, V, II, VI
    D. V, I, IV, VI, III, II   E. V, III, I, VI, IV, II

8. I. If, however, the rebuttal evidence presents an issue of credibility, it is for the jury to determine whether the presumption has, in fact, been destroyed.
    II. Once sufficient evidence to the contrary is introduced, the presumption disappears from the trial.
    III. The effect of a presumption is to place the burden upon the adversary to come forward with evidence to rebut the presumption.
    IV. When a presumption is overcome and ceases to exist in the case, the fact or facts which gave rise to the presumption still remain.
    V. Whether a presumption has been overcome is ordinarily a question for the court.
    VI. Such information may furnish a basis for a logical inference.
    The CORRECT answer is:
      A. IV, VI, II, V, I, III   B. III, II, V, I, IV, VI   C. V, III, VI, IV, II, I
      D. V, IV, I, II, VI, III   E. II, III, V, I, IV, VI

9. I. An executive may answer a letter by writing his reply on the face of the letter itself instead of having a return letter typed.
    II. This procedure is efficient because it saves the executive's time, the typist's time, and saves office file space.
    III. Copying machines are used in small offices as well as large offices to save time and money in making brief replies to business letters.
    IV. A copy is made on a copying machine to go into the company files, while the original is mailed back to the sender.
    The CORRECT answer is:
      A. I, II, IV, III   B. I, IV, II, III   C. III, I, IV, II   D. III, IV, II, I

10. I. Most organizations favor one of the types but always include the others to a lesser degree.
    II. However, we can detect a definite trend toward greater use of symbolic control.
    III. We suggest that our local police agencies are today primarily utilizing material control.
    IV. Control can be classified into three types: physical, material, and symbolic.
    The CORRECT answer is:
      A. IV, II, III, I   B. II, I, IV, III   C. III, IV, II, I   D. IV, I, III, II

11. I. Project residents had first claim to this use, followed by surrounding neighborhood children.
    II. By contrast, recreation space within the project's interior was found to be used more often by both groups.
    III. Studies of the use of project grounds in many cities showed grounds left open for public use were neglected and unused, both by residents and by members of the surrounding community.
    IV. Project residents had clearly laid claim to the play spaces, setting up and enforcing unwritten rules for use.
    V. Each group, by experience, found their activities easily disrupted by other groups, and their claim to the use of space for recreation difficult to enforce.

The CORRECT answer is:
A. IV, V, I, II, III
B. V, II, IV, III, I
C. I, IV, III, II, V
D. III, V, II, IV, I

12. I. They do not consider the problems correctable within the existing subsidy formula and social policy of accepting all eligible applicants regardless of social behavior.
    II. A recent survey, however, indicated that tenants believe these problems correctable by local housing authorities and management within the existing financial formula.
    III. Many of the problems and complaints concerning public housing management and design have created resentment between the tenant and the landlord.
    IV. This same survey indicated that administrators and managers do not agree with the tenants.
    The CORRECT answer is:
    A. II, I, III, IV   B. I, III, IV, II   C. III, II, IV, I   D. IV, II, I, III

13. I. In single-family residences, there is usually enough distance between tenants to prevent occupants from annoying one another.
    II. For example, a certain small percentage of tenant families has one or more members addicted to alcohol.
    III. While managers believe in the right of individuals to live as they choose, the manager becomes concerned when the pattern of living jeopardizes others' rights.
    IV. Still others turn night into day, staging lusty entertainments which carry on into the hours when most tenants are trying to sleep.
    V. In apartment buildings, however, tenants live so closely together that any misbehavior can result in unpleasant living conditions.
    VI. Other families engage in violent argument.
    The CORRECT answer is:
    A. III, II, V, IV, VI, I
    B. I, V, II, VI, IV, III
    C. II, V, IV, I, III, VI
    D. IV, II, V, VI, III, I

14. I. Congress made the commitment explicit in the Housing Act of 194, establishing as a national goal the realization of a *decent home and suitable environment for every American family*.
    II. The result has been that the goal of decent home and suitable environment is still as far distant as ever for the disadvantaged urban family.
    III. In spite of this action by Congress, federal housing programs have continued to be fragmented and grossly underfunded.
    IV. The passage of the National Housing Act signaled a few federal commitment to provide housing for the nation's citizens.
    The CORRECT answer is:
    A. I, IV, III, II   B. IV, I, III, II   C. IV, I, II, III   D. II, IV, I, III

15. I. The greater expense does not necessarily involve *exploitation*, but it is often perceived as exploitative and unfair by those who are aware of the price differences involved, but unaware of operating costs.
    II. Ghetto residents believe they are *exploited* by local merchants, and evidence substantiates some of these beliefs.
    III. However, stores in low-income areas were more likely to be small independents, which could not achieve the economies available to supermarket chains and were, therefore, more likely to charge higher prices, and the customers were more likely to buy smaller-sized packages which are more expensive per unit of measure.
    IV. A study conducted in one city showed that distinctly higher prices were charged for goods sold in ghetto stores in other areas.
    The CORRECT answer is:
      A. IV, II, I, III   B. IV, I, III, II   C. II, IV, III, I   D. II, III, IV, I

15.____

KEY (CORRECT ANSWERS)

1.	C	6.	C	11.	D
2.	E	7.	A	12.	C
3.	B	8.	B	13.	B
4.	B	9.	C	14.	B
5.	D	10.	D	15.	C

REPORT WRITING
EXAMINATION SECTION
TEST 1

DIRECTIONS: Each question or incomplete statement is followed by several suggested answers or completions. Select the one that BEST answers the question or completes the statement. *PRINT THE LETTER OF THE CORRECT ANSWER IN THE SPACE AT THE RIGHT.*

Questions 1-3.

DIRECTIONS: Questions 1 to 3 are based on the following example of a report. The report consists of ten numbered sentences, some of which are *not* consistent with the principles of good report writing.

(1) On the evening of February 24, Roscoe and Leroy, two members of the "Red Devils," were entering with a bottle of wine in their hands. (2) It was unusually good wine for these boys to buy, (3) I told them to give me the bottle and they refused, and added that they wouldn't let anyone "put them out." (4) I told them they were entitled to have a good time, but they could not do it the way they wanted; there were certain rules they had to observe. (5) At this point, Roscoe said he had seen me box at camp and suggested that Leroy not accept my offer. (6) Then I said firmly that the admission fee did not give them the authority to tell me what to do. (7) I also told them that, if they thought I would fight them over such a matter, they were sadly mistaken. (8) I added, however, that we could go to the gym right now and settle it another way if they wished. (9) Leroy immediately said that he was sorry, he had not understood the rules, and he did not want his quarter back. (10) On the other hand, they would not give up their bottle either, so they left the premises.

1. Only material that is relevant to the main thought of a report should be included. Which of the following sentences from the report contains material which is LEAST relevant to this report? Sentence
   "A. 2   B. 3   C. 8   D. 9

2. A good report should be arranged in logical order. Which of the following sentences from the report does NOT appear in its proper sequence in the report? Sentence
   A. 3   B. 5   C. 7   D. 9

3. Reports should include all essential information. Of the following, the MOST important fact that is *missing* from this report is:
   A. Who was involved in the incident   B. How the incident was resolved
   C. When the incident took place   D. Where the incident took place

4. The MOST serious of the following faults *commonly* found in explanatory reports is
   A. the use of slang terms   B. excessive details
   C. personal bias   D. redundancy

5. In reviewing a report he has prepared to submit to his superiors, a supervisor finds that his paragraphs are a typewritten page long and decides to make some revisions.
Of the following, the MOST important question he should ask about each paragraph is
   A. Are the words too lengthy?
   B. Is the idea under discussion too abstract?
   C. Is more than one central thought being expressed?
   D. Are the sentences too long?

5.____

6. The summary or findings of a long management report intended for the typical manager should, *generally*, appear _____ the report.
   A. at the very beginning of   B. at the end of
   C. throughout   D. in the middle of

6.____

7. In preparing a report that includes several tables, if not otherwise instructed, the typist should MOST properly include a list of tables
   A. in the introductory part of the report
   B. at the end of each chapter in the body of the report
   C. in the supplementary part of the report as an appendix
   D. in the supplementary part of the report as a part of the index

7.____

8. When typing a preliminary draft of a report, the one of the following which you should *generally* NOT do is to
   A. erase typing errors and deletions rather than "X"ing them out
   B. leave plenty of room at the top, bottom, and sides of each page
   C. make only the number of copies that you are asked to make
   D. type double or triple space

8.____

9. When you determine the methods of emphasis you will use in typing the titles, headings and subheadings of a report, the one of the following which it is MOST important to keep in mind is that
   A. all headings of the same rank should be typed in the same way
   B. all headings should be typed in the single style which is most pleasing to the eye
   C. headings should not take up more than one-third of the page width
   D. only one method should be used for all headings, whatever their rank

9.____

10. The one of the following ways in which inter-office memoranda *differ* from long formal reports is that they, *generally*,
    A. are written as if the reader is familiar with the vocabulary and technical background of the writer
    B. do not have a "subject line" which describes the major topic covered in the text
    C. include a listing of reference materials which support the memo writer's conclusions
    D. require that a letter of transmittal be attached

10.____

11. It is *preferable* to print information on a field report rather than write it out longhand MAINLY because
    A. printing takes less time to write than writing long hand
    B. printing is usually easier to read than longhand writing
    C. longhand writing on field reports is not acceptable in court cases
    D. printing occupies less space on a report than longhand writing

11.____

12. Of the following characteristics of a written report, the one that is MOST important is its
    A. length   B. accuracy   C. organization   D. grammar

12.____

13. A written report to your superior contains many spelling errors.
    Of the following statements relating to spelling errors, the one that is MOST NEARLY correct is that
    A. this is unimportant as long as the meaning of the report is clear
    B. readers of the report will ignore the many spelling errors
    C. readers of the report will get a poor opinion of the writer of the report
    D. spelling errors are unimportant as long as the grammar is correct

13.____

14. Written reports to your superior should have the same general arrangement and layout.
    The BEST reason for this requirement is that the
    A. report will be more accurate
    B. report will be more complete
    C. person who reads the report will know what the subject of the report is
    D. person who reads the report will know where to look for information in the report

14.____

15. The first paragraph of a report usually contains detailed information on the subject of the report.
    Of the following, the BEST reason for this requirement is to enable the
    A. reader to quickly find the subject of the report
    B. typist to immediately determine the subject of the report so that she will understand what she is typing
    C. clerk to determine to whom copies of the report will be needed
    D. typist to quickly determine how many copies of the report will be needed

15.____

16. Of the following statements concerning reports, the one which is LEAST valid is:
    A. A case report should contain factual material to support conclusions made
    B. An extremely detailed report may be of less value than a brief report giving the essential facts
    C. Highly technical language should be avoided as far as possible in preparing a report to be used at a court trial
    D. The position of the important facts in a report does not influence the emphasis placed on them by the reader

16.____

17. Suppose that you realize that you have made an error in a report that has been forwarded to another unit. You know that this error is not likely to be discovered for some time.
Of the following, the MOST advisable course of action for you to take is to
   A. approach the supervisor of the other unit on an informal basis, and ask him to correct the error
   B. say nothing about it since most likely one error will not invalidate the entire report
   C. tell your supervisor immediately that you have made an error so that it may be corrected, if necessary
   D. wait until the error is discovered and then admit that you had made it

17.____

18. In a report, words in a sentence must be arranged properly to make sure that the intended meaning of the sentence is clear.
The sentence below that does NOT make sense because a clause has been separated from the word on which its meaning depends is:
   A. To be a good writer, clarity is necessary.
   B. To be a good writer, you must write clearly.
   C. You must write clearly to be a good writer.
   D. Clarity is necessary to good writing.

18.____

19. The use of a graph to show statistical data in a report is *superior* to a table because it
   A. emphasizes approximations
   B. emphasizes facts and relationships more dramatically
   C. presents data more accurately
   D. is easily understood by the average reader

19.____

20. Of the following, the degree of formality required of a written report is, MOST likely to depend on the
   A. subject matter of the report
   B. frequency of its occurrence
   C. amount of time available for its preparation
   D. audience for whom the report is intended

20.____

Questions 21-25.

DIRECTIONS: Questions 21 through 25 consist of sets of four sentences lettered A, B, C, and D. For each question, choose the sentence which is grammatically and stylistically MOST appropriate for use in a formal written report.

21. A. It is recommended, therefore, that the impasse panel hearings are to be convened on September 30.
    B. It is therefore recommended that the impasse panel hearings be convened on September 30.
    C. Therefore, it is recommended to convene the impasse panel hearings on September 30.
    D. It is recommended that the impasse panel hearings therefore should be convened on September 30.

21.____

22. A. Penalties have been assessed for violating the Taylor Law by several unions.
    B. When they violated provisions of the Taylor Law, several unions were later penalized.
    C. Several unions have been penalized for violating provisions of the Taylor Law.
    D. Several unions' violating provisions of the Taylor Law resulted in them being penalized.

22.____

23. A. The number of disputes settled through mediation has increased significantly over the past two years.
    B. The number of disputes settled through mediation are increasing significantly over two-year periods.
    C. Over the past two years, through mediation, the number of disputes settled increased significantly.
    D. There is a significant increase over the past two years of the number of disputes settled through mediation.

23.____

24. A. The union members will vote to determine if the contract is to be approved.
    B. It is not yet known whether the union members will ratify the proposed contract.
    C. When the union members vote, that will determine the new contract.
    D. Whether the union members will ratify the proposed contract, it is not yet known.

24.____

25. A. The parties agreed to an increase in fringe benefits in return for greater work productivity.
    B. Greater productivity was agreed to be provided in return for increased fringe benefits.
    C. Productivity and fringe benefits are interrelated; the higher the former, the more the latter grows.
    D. The contract now provides that the amount of fringe benefits will depend upon the level of output by the workers.

25.____

KEY (CORRECT ANSWERS)

1.	A	11.	B
2.	B	12.	B
3.	D	13.	C
4.	C	14.	D
5.	C	15.	A
6.	A	16.	D
7.	A	17.	C
8.	A	18.	A
9.	A	19.	B
10.	A	20.	D

21.	B
22.	C
23.	A
24.	B
25.	A

TEST 2

DIRECTIONS: Each question or incomplete statement is followed by several suggested answers or completions. Select the one that BEST answers the question or completes the statement. *PRINT THE LETTER OF THE CORRECT ANSWER IN THE SPACE AT THE RIGHT.*

Questions 1-4.

DIRECTIONS: Questions 1 through 4 are to be answered on the basis of the following report which was prepared by a supervisor for inclusion in his agency's annual report.

Line #

1 On Oct. 13, I was assigned to study the salaries paid
2 to clerical employees in various titles by the city and by
3 private industry in the area.
4 In order to get the data I needed, I called Mr. Johnson at
5 the Bureau of the Budget and the payroll officers at X Corp.-
6 a brokerage house, Y Co. –an insurance company, and Z Inc. –
7 a publishing firm. None of them was available and I had to call
8 all of them again the next day.
9 When I finally got the information I needed, I drew up a
10 chart, which is attached. Note that not all of the companies I
11 contacted employed people at all the different levels used in the
12 city service.
13 The conclusions I draw from analyzing this information is
14 as follows: The city's entry-level salary is about average for
15 the region; middle-level salaries are generally higher in the
16 city government than in private industry; but salaries at the
17 highest levels in private industry are better than city em-
18 ployees' pay.

1. Which of the following criticisms about the style in which this report is written is MOST valid?
   A. It is too informal.
   B. It is too concise.
   C. It is too choppy.
   D. The syntax is too complex.

1.____

2. Judging from the statements made in the report, the method followed by this employee in performing his research was
   A. *good*; he contacted a representative sample of businesses in the area
   B. *poor*; he should have drawn more definite conclusions
   C. *good*; he was persistent in collecting information
   D. *poor*; he did not make a thorough study

2.____

3. One sentence in this report contains a grammatical error. This sentence *begins* on line number
   A. 4   B. 7   C. 10   D. 13

3.____

4. The type of information given in this report which should be presented in footnotes or in an appendix, is the
   A. purpose of the study
   B. specifics about the businesses contacted
   C. reference to the chart
   D. conclusions drawn by the author

5. Of the following, a DISTINGUISHING characteristic of a written report intended for the head of your agency as compared to a report prepared for a lower-echilon staff member is that the report for the agency head should, *usually*, include
   A. considerably more detail, especially statistical data
   B. the essential details in an abbreviated form
   C. all available source material
   D. an annotated bibliography

6. Assume that you are asked to write a lengthy report for use by the administrator of your agency, the subject of which is "The Impact of Proposed New Data Processing Operations on Line Personnel" in your agency. You decide that the *most* appropriate type of report for you to prepare is an analytical report, including recommendations.
   The MAIN reason for your decision is that
   A. the subject of the report is extremely complex
   B. large sums of money are involved
   C. the report is being prepared for the administrator
   D. you intend to include charts and graphs

7. Assume that you are preparing a report based on a survey dealing with the attitudes of employees in Division X regarding proposed new changes in compensating employees for working overtime. Three percent of the respondents to the survey voluntarily offer an unfavorable opinion on the method of assigning overtime work, a question not specifically asked of the employees. On the basis of this information, the MOST appropriate and significant of the following comments for you to make in the report with regard to employees' attitudes on assigning overtime work is that
   A. an insignificant percentage of employees dislike the method of assigning overtime work
   B. three percent of the employees in Division X dislike the method of assigning overtime work
   C. three percent of the sample selected for the survey voiced an unfavorable opinion on the method of assigning overtime work
   D. some employees voluntarily voiced negative feelings about the method of assigning overtime work, making it impossible to determine the extent of this attitude

8. Assume that you have been asked to prepare a narrative summary of the monthly reports submitted by employees in your division.
   In preparing your summary of this month's reports, the FIRST step to take is to
   A. read through the reports, noting their general content and any unusual features
   B. decide how many typewritten pages your summary should contain
   C. make a written summary of each separate report, so that you will not have to go back to the original reports again
   D. ask each employee which points he would prefer to see emphasized in your summary

8._____

9. Assume that an administrative officer is writing a brief report to his superior outlining the advantages of matrix organization.
   Of the following, it would be INCORRECT to state that
   A. in matrix organization, a project is emphasized by designating one individual as the focal point for all matters pertaining to it
   B. utilization of manpower can be flexible in matrix organization because reservoir of specialists is maintained in the line operations
   C. the usual line-staff management is generally reversed in matrix organization
   D. in matrix organization, responsiveness to project needs is generally faster due to establishing needed communication lines and decision points

9._____

10. Written reports dealing with inspections of work and installations SHOULD be
    A. as long and detailed as practicable
    B. phrased with personal interpretations
    C. limited to the important facts of the inspection
    D. technically phrased to create an impression on superiors

10._____

11. It is important to use definite, exact words in preparing a descriptive report and to avoid, as much as possible, nouns that have vague meanings and, possibly, a different meaning for the reader than for the author.
    Which of the following sentences contains only nouns that are *definite* and *exact*?
    A. The free enterprise system should be vigorously encouraged in the United States.
    B. Arley Swopes climbed Mount Everest three times last year.
    C. Beauty is a characteristic of all the women at the party.
    D. Gil Noble asserts that he is a real democrat.

11._____

12. One way of shortening n unnecessarily long report is to reduce sentence length by eliminating the use of several words where a single one that does not alter the meaning will do.
    Which of the following sentences CANNOT be shortened without losing some of its information content?
    A. After being polished, the steel ball bearings ran at maximum speed.
    B. After the close of the war, John Taylor was made the recipient of a pension.
    C. In this day and age, you can call anyone up on the telephone.
    D. She is attractive in appearance, but she is a rather selfish person.

12._____

13. Employees are required to submit written reports of all unusual occurrences promptly.
    The BEST reason for such promptness is that the
    A. report may be too long if made at one's convenience
    C. report will tend to be more accurate as to facts
    D. employee is likely to make a better report under pressure

14. In making a report, it is poor practice to erase information on the report in order to make a change because
    A. there may be a question of what was changed and why it was changed
    B. you are likely to erase through the paper and tear the report
    C. the report will no longer look neat and presentable
    D. the duplicate copies will be smudged

15. The one of the following which BEST describes a periodic report is that it
    A. provides a record of accomplishments for a given time span and a comparison with similar time spans in the past
    B. covers the progress made in a project that has been postponed
    C. integrates, summarizes, and, perhaps, interprets published data on technical or scientific material
    D. describes a decision, advocates a policy or action, and presents facts in support of the writer's position

16. The PRIMARY purpose of including pictorial illustrations in a formal report is *usually* to
    A. amplify information which has been adequately treated verbally
    B. present details that are difficult to describe verbally
    C. provide the reader with a pleasant, momentary distraction
    D. present supplementary information incidental to the main ideas developed in the report

KEY (CORRECT ANSWERS)

1.	A		6.	A
2.	D		7.	D
3.	D		8.	A
4.	B		9.	C
5.	B		10.	C

11.	B.
12.	A.
13.	C
14.	A.
15.	A.
16	B.

www.ingramcontent.com/pod-product-compliance
Lightning Source LLC
Chambersburg PA
CBHW082209300426
44117CB00016B/2728